JOURNALISM
AND PR

RISJ CHALLENGES

CHALLENGES present findings, analysis and recommendations from Oxford's Reuters Institute for the Study of Journalism. The Institute is dedicated to the rigorous, international comparative study of journalism, in all its forms and on all continents. CHALLENGES muster evidence and research to take forward an important argument, beyond the mere expression of opinions. Each text is carefully reviewed by an editorial committee, drawing where necessary on the advice of leading experts in the relevant fields. CHALLENGES remain, however, the work of authors writing in their individual capacities, not a collective expression of views from the Institute.

EDITORIAL COMMITTEE

The editorial advisers on this CHALLENGE were Tim Burt and Rasmus Kleis Nielsen.

Funding for this Challenge was kindly provided by David Ure.

JOURNALISM AND PR

NEWS MEDIA AND PUBLIC RELATIONS IN THE DIGITAL AGE

JOHN LLOYD AND LAURA TOOGOOD

REUTERS
INSTITUTE for the
STUDY of
JOURNALISM

Published by I.B.Tauris & Co. Ltd in association with
the Reuters Institute for the Study of Journalism, University of Oxford

Published in 2015 by I.B.Tauris & Co. Ltd
London · New York
Reprinted in 2015
www.ibtauris.com

ISBN: 978 1 78453 062 4
eISBN: 978 0 85773 741 0

A full CIP record for this book is available from the British Library
A full CIP record is available from the Library of Congress

Library of Congress Catalog Card Number: available

Typeset by Riverside Publishing Solutions, Salisbury SP4 6NQ
Printed and bound by TJ International Ltd, Padstow, Cornwall

Contents

Executive Summary

The most notable observation to emerge from the research done here is the diminution of public relations' dependence on journalism, and the growth of journalism's dependence on PR. PR still needs journalism, which has always acted as a 'third-party endorsement' of its claims. But now it has other, often more powerful allies.

Allied to that is the confidence on the part of many PR leaders that they can take over, and are taking over, many of the functions of journalism, and of the media in general. 'Every organisation is a media organisation' has developed from being a slogan into becoming a growing reality.

The internet is the largest source of the shifts we now see between the complementary trades of journalism and public relations. The ease of access to it, its vast memory, and its huge data banks make all activities more transparent, pushing all organisations to greater openness. Social media increases transparency – and opens up an infinite demand for engagement at every level, from mighty corporations to the individual. This puts a high premium on a constant flow of messages from prominent institutions and individuals, proactively and reactively.

A large new area has opened up for public relations – in protecting and burnishing the reputation of companies, institutions, and individuals. Though always part of PR, reputation is now seen to be more fragile, more open to attack, especially on social media. New techniques of guarding reputation on the internet have been developed.

Corporations take part in the debates that concern them and speak to their business, including issues in the political and social spheres. The greater doubts about the efficacy and equity of the free market and of globalisation have impelled some leaders to enter the public arena, arguing both for the social and economic utility of their enterprises and for the viability of the free market system as a whole. The time when corporations proved their bona fides by displaying corporate social responsibility is being replaced with a call for an engagement with all stakeholders on the nature of their business, seeking to prove its social value and its ethical conduct.

Trust in, and the reputation of, public and private organisations and leaders is seen as more precarious than ever before – in large part the outcome of transparency and social media. The search for trust and the strategies developed to restore it in turn put a high premium on truth, and the development of a more consciously ethical posture. The need to protect and project the reputation of institutions gives public relations practitioners a greater prominence and status. The counsel of consultants – interpreting social and other trends and experienced in relations with the various stakeholders and constituencies which now surround companies, institutions, and people of prominence – is seen as more essential.

The stress on ethics for clients naturally leads to a reflection on real or alleged lack of ethics among PR executives themselves. This in turn leads to a stronger and more strongly voiced disapproval of those firms – particularly in London – which represent foreign states or individuals whose record, especially the record on human rights, is generally criticised.

The British royal family has been a central element for public relations in the UK for much of the present monarch's reign, and this is likely to become more crucial for her successor. The media sophistication of Britain's royal family is a barometer of how clients for all types of reputation management are now changing their approach to media-engagement. Reputations are no longer won or lost in a daily dialogue between PR agents and their media counterparts. Instead, in the second decade of the twenty-first century, both sides are redefining their roles – and their business models – for a new information age in which neither exercises the strategies and tactics they deployed in the past.

The US is the undisputed leader in political communications, and its techniques based on the use of large data sets allow it to individualise voters and speak more directly to their interests and demands. Political journalism in the US and elsewhere is now declining in newspapers and broadcast bulletins. Specialist publications and sites speak to niches and there is much more information available from actors in the political sphere than before. The legacy media are slowly ceding ground to specialist sites and individual journalist brands. Some of these retain a commitment to political neutrality; more do not.

As corporations are being impelled into an area of constant conversation, they both seek a larger quasi-political role and engage more directly and constantly with government at every level.

Acknowledgements

Thanks are due first of all to David Ure, whose generosity in funding the research has enabled this study both to range widely and to take the time needed to understand something of the state of relations between two trades at once antagonistic and mutually dependent.

We must also thank our many interviewees, some of whom are quoted by name, others who did not wish to be identified. Thanks are also due to the staff of the Reuters Institute for the Study of Journalism and I.B.Tauris for the editorial and other work on the drafts.

Notes on the Text

The research was done jointly by John Lloyd and Laura Toogood and supported by David Ure. John Lloyd wrote Chapters 1–3 and 5–6; Laura Toogood wrote Chapter 4.

Chapter 1 is a brief and selective history of PR; Chapter 2, on corporate PR; Chapter 3, on political communications; Chapter 4, a guide to how public relations uses the internet and social media; Chapter 5, a comparison of US/UK public relations and political communications with the practice of these arts in China, Russia, and France.

We have relied mainly on interviews with practitioners, most of whom are public relations and political communications professionals. PR professionals are naturally good at presenting themselves: we have checked on some, but by no means all, of their claims.

The main works consulted are cited in the references: we did not engage with most of the large academic literature on public relations and political communications.

In the course of this book, we cite the *Financial Times* several times and the online reputation business Digitalis a few times. John Lloyd was a domestic and foreign correspondent for the *FT* for more than 20 years and is a (non-staff) Contributing Editor. Laura Toogood is Managing Director of Private Clients at Digitalis.

Introduction

Public relations can claim venerable status as a natural offspring of human intercourse, and many of its practitioners refer to that status as evidence of the ordinary, human nature of their work. In a speech in Melbourne in 2013, the former director of communications for Prime Minister Tony Blair, Alastair Campbell, said, 'There has always been comm[unication]s. There has always been public affairs. There has always been PR. There has always been spin. Read the Bible for heaven's sake.'[1]

We are concerned with the industry: Campbell's comment is about the pre-industrial roots, the way in which people – especially those with power – sought to influence others by speech and images, rather than force or threats. The Bible *is* a large source for this all-embracing view of PR. Much of the New Testament is concerned with ascribing to Jesus the status of a god, through recounting his miraculous birth, resurrection after crucifixion, and the miracles he wrought between these two events. Is the Bible public relations? It has certainly been stunningly successful in relating to large numbers of publics.

Yet it is disingenuous to equate that with the public relations machines which now exist. The first type of influencing is the public face adopted by movements of every kind – religious, military, political – as well as individual desires and needs, and to be successful requires belief, skill, plausibility, and often at least the threat of retribution within the framework of societies bound by tradition and ritual.

The second type is an ever-larger presence in government, commercial, and cultural life; it grew and now exists in societies where specialised services are a large part of the economy and where most economies depend largely on markets. These require widely available information to encourage commercial activity (buying and selling) and need the broad diffusion of government information and persuasion at every administrative level, directly in the form of advertising, both directly and indirectly in the case of public relations. And as the presiding genius of PR, Edward Bernays, believed, public relations became more necessary in societies which had lost much of the guidance of tradition and ritual.

Journalism, not much older as an organised profession than public relations, has come to depend on it even as it scorns it. That dependence is not less today: in some cases, it is greater.

1

Public Relations: A Brief Selective History

Bernays, a nephew of Sigmund Freud, did not invent public relations, but he was the first to think through both its operational necessities and procedures, and – in a series of writings – to reflect on its place in society and the tasks which he believed the developing society presented to it.

Urban society, he thought, bred individualism: he wrote that in the cities of Greece, 'with the increase in the status and power of the individual came a refusal to accept blindly the untrammelled authority of nobility and the pronouncements of religion' (Bernays 2011). Public opinion, he wrote, had been in embryo in Greek and Roman societies but blossomed just before and during the French Revolution and in the Enlightenment.

He quotes Abraham Lincoln's remark – during one of his 1858 debates with the Democratic Presidential candidate Stephen Douglas, in Ottawa (Illinois) – that 'public sentiment is everything. With public sentiment nothing can fail. Without it nothing can succeed' (manifestly wrong: disastrous wars and failed grand projects have been powered by public sentiment).

Democratic mass societies must have leaders who campaign actively for their policies – who 'engineer consent' as Bernays (1947) put it. The phrase has acquired a pejorative connotation, and has haunted Bernays's memory ever since.

He seems to have meant it in two ways. One was that there could and should be an identity of interest between capital and labour, governing and governed: and that identity must be 'engineered' by public relations, since public approval is essential for every large project. But the people should take part in freely debating the large issues, since this 'engineering … is the very essence of the democratic process, the freedom to persuade and suggest'. Public relations, in its early days as in its later ones, has as one of its public justifications that it can replace *force majeure* with negotiation and agreement.

No PR executive would use such a phrase today: and the imperative which Bernays and others genuinely believed lay behind the development of the trade – that a society of individuals will fall into chaos if consent is not engineered – is not presently part of the lexicon of mature democratic societies, though it is in developing ones. Today, however, PR agents increasingly do take a lead from Bernays when they promise to protect a client's 'licence to operate'.

PR as social democracy

Bernays's assumption is that the 'engineering', especially by government, is done for the public's own good, and that it is a matter of getting the public to understand and accept it. This was not a rogue idea: indeed, it was derived from President Theodore Roosevelt himself, whom Bernays mentions approvingly in *Crystallizing Public Opinion* (2011) as one of the first politicians to use public relations as a means of achieving progressive ends – he argued in the Congress that 'much can be done by the government in labour matters merely by giving publicity to certain conditions' (he had in mind the condition of miners, which had been publicised in the Colorado mining strike of that year).

This view – that the state could be a force for the righting of wrongs and for the civic education of ordinary people – was a popular one, especially on the democratic left, for much of the twentieth century: and it lay behind a significant part of early public relations, in the US and especially in the UK, and later elsewhere.

It is a long way from public relations' present reputation (though not its practice) that some of its roots are as much in leftist politics as in capitalist corporations. In a study of the development of PR in the UK, Scott Anthony (2008) writes that, in the 1920s and 1930s, when the profession was establishing itself in the UK, it was 'driven by a progressive faction [...] Public relations [...] was an imaginative process of arbitration which wove competing demands into a form which best served a bureaucratic definition of the national interest.'

The conception of many of the profession's early leaders in the two largest anglophone countries was that their task was as much to inform citizens of their rights and to convince them of what was good for them as it was to stimulate desires for products and services.

An outstanding example was the work, in documentary film in the UK and later in Canada, of John Grierson, which sprang from this belief in the educative, even liberating, effect of public relations. Grierson, like Bernays before him, was seized by the idea – which he took from the US writer Walter Lippmann's 1922 book *Public Opinion* – that democracy was threatened by the complexity of modern life, which effectively 'disenfranchised' most people because they could not understand the society and the politics of which, allegedly, they were the democratic masters. The antidote, he believed, was a popular press which explained complex issues clearly: and the new popular medium, film.

In both the US and the UK at least, politicians believed that clear, popularly presented information would radically change behaviour and mould new citizens. Both Presidents Theodore (1901–9) and Franklin Delano (1933–45) Roosevelt believed it, and took a close interest in furthering it. The post-war Labour government in the UK thought it was creating a new, socialist, moral society: for that, as the prime minister Clement Attlee told his 1948 conference, society needed 'a higher standard of civic virtue than capitalism. It demands a conscious and active participation in public affairs.'

Stephen Taylor, a senior government aide, wrote in *The Times* in October 1945 that 'if [the citizen] is to know what Parliament has done in his name, and what part he has in the post-war social structure, he must be told and told repeatedly in language he can understand. This is not socialist propaganda but simply a condition of the survival of democracy' (quoting Jay 1937).

Thus the government created and expanded the role of public relations in its departments, and through the Central Office of Information. As it came under greater pressure from a population impatient at the continuation of wartime controls and rationing, and as the novelty of and gratitude for innovations like the National Health Service wore thinner, the tempo of the 'explanations' of government policy speeded up: according to Martin Moore in his study of the period, 'as the communication increases in complexity and becomes more staged, so it shifts further from its original essence and becomes less democratically justifiable. Presentation is consciously separated from policy and communication becomes less about informing and explaining and more about persuading and directing' (2006).

The PR executive as the reporter's friend

Walter Lippmann, who was a respected authority in the interwar and post-war periods on public policy and the role of the media, saw that journalism was not a matter of reporting 'the facts' but of reporting what he called a 'stylized' version of them – that is, the facts given a narrative shape. In a passage in his *Public Opinion* (1997), he writes of the issue of bad working conditions (in this case at Pittsburgh Steel) to argue that to make a proper accounting of the conditions would take a team of investigators, many days of research, and 'fat volumes' of print. Newspapers could not attempt such a project, and thus 'the bad conditions as such are not news, because in all but exceptional cases, journalism is not a first hand report of the raw material. It is a report of that material after it has been stylized [i.e. given a narrative shape]'.

If journalism is 'the first draft of history' then public relations is the first draft's first draft. Lippmann provides a firm base for public relations, by rooting it in the needs of hard-pressed newspapermen and women, seeking with too little time to fit too many stories into spaces too exiguous for too much complexity. He also makes it clear that the 'publicity man', taking a fee from a client, cannot be expected to be other than his mouthpiece.

> Since, in respect to most of the big topics of news, facts are not simple, and [...] it is natural that everyone should wish to make his own choice of facts for the newspaper to print. The publicity man does that [...] But it follows that the picture which the publicity man makes for the reporter is the one he wishes the public to see. He is censor and propagandist, responsible only to his employers, and to the whole truth responsible only as it accords with the employer's conception of his own interest.
>
> The development of the publicity man is a clear sign that the facts of modern life do not spontaneously take a shape in which they can be known. They must be given a shape by somebody ... (Lippmann 1997)

Giving newspaper reporters and editors comprehensible narratives was the main – for some the only – job of the PR man for much of the twentieth century: Tim Burt, one of the most acute of today's UK practitioners, writes that 'for most of the last century, PR was built on the simple tasks of salesmanship and persuasion, underpinned by feudal loyalty to clients' (2012).

The PR executive as stunt man

The 'feudal loyalty' – which Burt and others would claim is much lessened today – was evident in the early practitioners, including Bernays, who, 'hired to sell a product or service, instead sold whole new ways of behaving' (Tye 1998). These varied from the small to the large: tasked by the hairnet company Venida, hit by new fashions for short hair, Bernays started a campaign for women at work to wear nets both to stop it being caught in machinery, and to keep it out of food products; on the other side, he paid leading actresses to endorse the beauty of long hair.

Ivy Lee, a Princeton-educated Methodist minister's son from Georgia, is usually bracketed with Bernays as a founding pioneer of the trade. Like Bernays, his actions – and thus his reputation – have light and dark sides. He could be ruthless in putting out one-sided, even mendacious material; yet he sought to persuade clients of the need for more openness, and even for better conditions for their workers. In the 1920s, he sought to portray the Soviet Union in a positive light; in the 1930s, he worked to advise the German chemical company IG Farben on how to moderate the bad press which the Nazi regime received: not for the first or last time in his use of this form of rationale, Lee argued that he was working through the company to persuade Hitler to reform.

Lee was credited (at least by himself) as having told the heir to the Standard Oil fortune to 'tell the truth because sooner or later the public will find out anyway' – advice which is the more resonant today, as we'll see. He's routinely cited as one of the largest influences on PR – sometimes credited with being more powerful, through his work in mending broken reputations and in handling crises, than Bernays.

Both Bernays and Lee knew that they had to attract the attention of the press. Thus they organised visits, shows, and stunts which made news, ensuring that the client or the product became part of journalism, rather than advertising. This basic practice has been followed ever since: only now is it changing, though not disappearing.

The PR executive as counsellor

Although public relations often proclaims its entrepreneurial lineage, it owes a good deal to state activism, and to disasters. In *Crystallizing Public Opinion*, Bernays credits Teddy Roosevelt's policies, but also the use of

7

propaganda (not then a pejorative) in the First World War, and the financial crash of the late 1920s which 'destroyed the voice of business – and gave great acceleration to professional public relations activity'.

Neither Lee nor Bernays left large companies as their legacies: the rapid postwar growth was based on US firms like Burson-Marsteller, founded by the PR man Harold Burson and the advertising man William Marsteller; Hill & Knowlton, with its roots in the 1930s, founded by John Hill, a former financial writer, and Donald Knowlton, a bank's PR man; and Edelman, founded by the former sports reporter Daniel Edelman (now run by his son Richard).[1]

The most successful PR executives have ever been those who could forge a strong relationship with one at or close to the top of the organisation they were promoting. In some industries – especially those exposed to the public gaze, such as consumer products companies – this takes the form of an the in-house communications chief or the head of an agency contracted to the company.

The rise of the flack

Political communications grew in parallel to corporate PR, and can be close to their corporate brethren, with personnel shifting between the two continually: Burson-Marsteller, for example, has been headed in the past decade by Mark Penn and Don Baer, both of whom worked in communications at the Clinton White House. Jake Siewert, now at Goldman Sachs, was also a White House veteran. The techniques both differ and coincide. The flack – so-called because he absorbs incoming fire from political journalists – has, at least in the US, become much more powerful in the past two decades, as the political parties have declined and the need for media strategies has become central.

Like public relations, too, it is as old as the trade on which it depends: where there has been politics, there have been fixers, seeking to smooth the way for policies, denigrate opponents, and give shape to the central figure's programme and appeal. James Harding (2008: 6) sees the trade as a 'business opportunity [existing] in the shortcomings of politicians', and locates an early practitioner in democratic times in the London-born John Beckley, who 'was one of the first to go negative: he claimed George Washington had stolen public funds and called for his impeachment'.

The better, the worse

The more sophisticated PR became, the more it was seen as acting unambiguously for the worse. A slew of books which grappled with the great spread of PR and political consulting in the 1950s and into the 1960s – as corporations took on larger and larger PR staffs and first the Republicans and then the Democrats hired increasingly expensive advisers to their campaigns – looked at the changes with deeply hostile eyes. This view of PR and political communications has remained strong, though it has somewhat diminished now as PR becomes more powerful and ubiquitous, and is used by non-governmental organisations with humanitarian and liberal aims.

Among the earliest of these works was Vance Packard's influential 1957 polemic, *The Hidden Persuaders*: in it, he described how 'political hucksters' were now treating voters as spectator-consumers, not much interested in politics or its content, able to be roused only by controversy, stunts and personality. This approach seemed justified, Packard wrote, 'by the growing evidence that voters could not be depended on to be rational. There seemed to be a strong illogical or non-logical element in their behaviour, both individually and in masses' (Packard 2007).

As Packard discovered in his research, this had been happily accepted by the commercial world which was abreast of the new approach – and which was exporting its techniques to the political communicators. He quotes an editorial in an early 1956 edition of the magazine *The Nation's Business*, published by the US Chamber of Commerce, which reported:

> *Both parties will merchandise their candidates and issues by the same methods that business has developed to sell goods [...] no flag-waving faithfuls will parade the streets. Instead corps of volunteers will ring doorbells and telephones [...] radio spot announcements and ads will repeat phrases with a planned intensity. Billboards will push slogans of proven power [...] candidates need [...] to look 'sincerely at the TV camera'.* (Packard 2007)

It was an early intimation of the replacement of political parties (the 'faithfuls') by public relations, a movement which has since advanced.

The same year, a retired advertising executive, John Schneider, wrote *The Golden Kazoo* (1956), a novel which with a fair degree of prescience described the 1960 election, where the image-makers have taken over, viewing candidates as 'the merchandise' and the electorate as 'the market'. Schneider pictures the winning candidate as having a pregnant wife: Jackie Kennedy learned she was pregnant (with John F. Kennedy junior) shortly after the 1960 presidential election campaign began.

Television was the game changer here: it was kind to John Kennedy in 1960, harsh on the more experienced Richard Nixon: in his *The Powers That Be*, the chronicler of this period, David Halberstam (2000), wrote that Kennedy was the first successful product of a politics which thought about their candidate in televisual terms, rather than only in terms of party loyalty, or length of experience, or even policy positions. The intellectuals and academics, and many in politics and journalism, saw this trend as more or less uniformly bad: most magisterially, the historian Daniel Boorstin, Librarian of Congress 1975–87, wrote in *The Image* (1997) that advertising allied to the media, especially television, had flooded the public sphere with 'pseudo events', happenings which are created by advertising people or journalists for the purpose of being reported or reproduced. 'The question: "is it real?" is less important than "is it newsworthy?"' (Boorstin 1997).

In a sustained piece of passionate writing at the end of his book, Boorstin writes:

> *we are threatened by a new and peculiarly American menace [...] the menace of unreality. The threat of nothingness is the danger of replacing American dreams by American illusions [...] we are the most illusioned people on earth. Yet we dare not become disillusioned because our illusions are the very house in which we live; they are our news, our heroes, our adventure, our forms of art, our very experience.* (1997)

In sum

- PR has, since it took on an organised form, been split between differing objectives – engineering social and political outcomes, persuading both the masses and specific stakeholder groups, mediating between opposing groups, and providing a service to the public.
- PR executives have always sought to give a coherent and accessible account of events, personalities, and institutions, formed in part from

the facts, in part from the need to attract attention and to persuade, in part from the demands of the client.

- PR executives have always tried to get close to and to influence the heads of the institutions for which they work – and they have always tried to get close to and attract the interest of the news media. Political communications use many of the same techniques – and political communicators are necessarily always very close to the politician or official for whom they work.
- PR has always attracted odium, often from journalists, who depend on it most. From the 1950s, this took a stronger form in the writings of commentators and sociologists, often of the left, who saw the profession as mendacious and manipulative, a view which has remained.

2

Corporate PR

Transparency engenders truth

No lipstick for pigs

Corporate public relations is PR's major form, even if less obviously dramatisable than political communications. It is not a huge business – the influential Holmes Report's estimate for 2014 reveals an industry worldwide of an estimated 80,000 people working in agencies and a total income of $12.5bn.[1] But it is growing strongly presently – at around 8% a year, a rate sustained for the past three years. This does not count the many thousands of PR people working within companies, banks, governments, and institutions.

In his Trend Forecast for 2014,[2] Paul Holmes – the eponymous report's founder and main author – picks out elements which feature in our essay. Social media, he believes, will come into their own in this year – the year 'in which savvy and sophisticated corporate communicators come to understand that digital and social media provide them with an opportunity to tell their corporate stories more proactively, to realize competitive advantage by walking the walk rather than just talking the talk'.

The 'walking the talk' theme is the dominant one, Holmes believes, quoting a range of senior PR executives. 'Walking the talk will be an even more important factor in the corporate arena,' says Ciro Dias Reis, CEO of Brazilian agency Imagem Corporativa. 'That means companies really acting as their speeches suggest'. According to Hill+Knowlton US president and CEO Andy Weitz: 'We define character as the intersection – and ultimately, the alignment – of a company's brand, reputation and behaviour. Communicating character means breaking down the barriers between the teams that manage a company's brand, its behaviour and the public's perceptions of it.'

It is one of the received wisdoms in PR that 'putting lipstick on a pig' does not work. Tim (Lord) Bell, co-founder of Bell Pottinger, has a story, less obscure than Andy Weitz's pronouncement, to illuminate it:

> *Someone asked me to take on Naomi Campbell, who wanted to be seen as nice. Her agent said – give me a position strategy. I said: the most unpleasant fashion model in the world. She said: she's that already. I said, sure, that's her position strategy, what are you worrying about? It hasn't stopped her making money and doing what she wants to do. So I said to her – tell her to be nicer and stop being nasty.*

Bell does not always live up to the moral of his story: he has represented and represents clients whose reputations were substantially worse than that of a foul-tempered model, and has used his skill to represent them as at least striving to do better. But it is a humorous recognition that the essence of a bad client will usually come through sooner or later. This was thought to be the case for a century: Ivy Lee's advice to 'tell the truth because sooner or later the public will find out anyway' has not always been taken and was not by him, but it was at least a component in PR thinking and a certain inhibition. Now, Lee's dictum has become holy writ. Transparency, and the shifts in corporate behaviour it dictates, is a main marketing tool of public relations: it is a large new area in which the expertise of PR consultants, in interpreting the demands of a new environment to company leaders, can be deployed.

The theme is now pervasive: in political communication as in corporate PR. Because it is important, we tried in the course of our interviews to probe the many declarations of executives that truth and transparency are winning out, by making clear the limits under which PR works. This is not to say such claims are, prima facie, false: the pressures of both digital technology and of public opinion *are* pushing the trade in the direction of greater frankness, after, if not always before, the event. But they depend on the power and influence of the PR executive to convince his or her clients or bosses that transparency means there should be greater conformity between the expressed aims of the organisation represented and its quotidian behaviour.

It is a very large claim: as most would admit when the issue is put to them, they work for a client, or a boss, and if the client or boss wishes to be represented in a way in which the PR executive judges to be inappropriate, the choices are one of the two meanings of the word resignation. But it cannot be dismissed: social media, especially, can focus attention on that which, before they became ubiquitous, would have remained hidden.

Clay Shirky (2008) tells the story of a woman named Ivanna who left an expensive cellphone in a New York City taxi: she offered a reward for its return in a text which would be displayed on the phone. The girl who had found it took pictures of her friends with it, and these showed up on a new phone Ivanna had purchased because her phone company transferred the information from the old to the new; she thus was able to trace it. Ivanna emailed the finder – named Sasha – and asked for the phone to be returned. Sasha, who is Hispanic, emailed back saying her 'white ass' didn't deserve to have it returned. Ivanna's friend, Evan, created a web page which described what had happened, and put it up on his website. It got some attention, was picked up by the collaborative news site Digg, and attracted much more: people took Ivanna's side, and some worked out who Sasha was, and where she lived. The NYPD became involved, and finally the phone was reluctantly returned.

The publicising of a story which was easy to understand, had happened in some form to most people, offended many people's sense of justice, and stimulated their hunting instincts meant that what would have been a defeat for Ivanna was turned into a win, with Sasha humiliated. The creation of an audience through social media was the key to the happy outcome, but social media alone did not create it. Sasha's bad behaviour became transparent because the audience, or part of it, became activists: they pursued the leads supplied by Evan, put pressure on Sasha, and finally won the involvement of an NYPD which would certainly, absent the publicity, have at best filed it as missing.

The transparency and greater honesty which PR executives proclaim is not as if brick walls everywhere have suddenly become glass. The internet and social media put millions of issues into the public domain, of which a few will receive the benison – or the curse – of a viral circulation. Often (though not in Ivanna's phone's case) it will depend on the form of the media. An episode in the US political drama series *House of Cards* neatly caught this: a US congressman, running for governor while in the early stages of recovering from alcoholism, slipped off the wagon and gave a drunken interview to a small radio station. It might have been ignored – but a fast-growing news website was directed by the Borgia-like politician at the centre of the series to do a story on it, from there it was picked up by the *New York Times*, and the congressman, who might have survived, was finished. The cycle, of minor mainstream media to growing new media to still-major mainstream media, well captures something of the new hierarchies of media influence, as well as demonstrating what it takes for an action to become 'transparent'.

As Evgeny Morozov emphasises in his many writings, social media can only do so much, and can be used for many different and conflicting ends. For transparency to be a result, the media need people to take an interest, and *do* something – or at any rate react in some way. A PR agency, or more likely an agency's client, can 'get away with' dubious dealings and false claims in the internet age: but will be punished, sometimes very hard, if media fuse with a crowd, and the crowd uses the media to create a storm of protest or revulsion.

No PR leader we spoke to said other than that 'transparency' was revolutionising both their business, and that of their clients. There are pockets of business – private equity is one in the financial area – where, according to Roland Rudd, head of the Finsbury agency, an exposure to the media is a choice rather than a necessity. Rudd also says, with others, that he is often hired to keep clients out of the media, which seems to point to the fact that transparency can be avoided. But for big corporations with a large public exposure, especially those in the media and consumer sectors, increased transparency and the need for more disclosure seems, at present, an inexorable trend.

Ed Williams, the UK head of Edelman who spent some years as Director of Communications at the BBC, gives an example of the pressures for more openness:

> *The BBC was faced with rising public disquiet about salaries and pension pay-outs – we in communications saw that the public wanted the Corporation to be run in a transparent way. It had to get ahead of the game on this. And so we decided to publish its top salaries and pension payments.*
>
> *The decision went down badly with senior executives. But we took the decision that it was better to publish the salaries, even against the wishes of senior colleagues. The job of the communications function is to see what's coming from around the corner; to look into the future and see what will get bigger.*

Williams notes the limits:

> *You cannot go too far down the moral road, though – to argue that you cannot represent a drinks company because drink is bad for you; an oil*

company because it destroys the environment; or an airline company because it's polluting [...] yet increasingly public relations will be at the centre of a public debate, and it will have to argue its position, case by case.

Alastair Campbell, the director of communications for Tony Blair and later a consultant for Portman PR, founded and run by his former deputy, Tim Allen, says that 'Lies have always been out – but what *was* done was to put out a version of the truth which is at the same time not really accurate – people thought that would pass and it often did – but now it's the intensity of the scrutiny which stops that.'

Scrubbing down the malefactors

There's a paradoxical service which journalists – nearly always well-known TV journalists or presenters – now implicitly offer corporations: and this is, to haul their chief executives over the coals of an abrasive interview and, by humbling, cleanse them. Sumeet Desai, a former Reuters economics and politics reporter, now Head of Public Affairs for the much-battered Royal Bank of Scotland, instances the row which broke over the head of the bank's CEO, Stephen Hester, in 2012, when he was offered a bonus of nearly £1m, this after the bank had been bailed out by the taxpayer to the tune of £50bn.

His bonus of just under £1m had caused an almighty row, making him almost a household name. At first the reaction here was – well, he's taken it now; let's move away from it. But what we decided was that we must do it head on, so he should go on to BBC Radio 4's Today programme, do the BBC1 Andrew Marr Show, say: these are the reasons I'm doing this. There was quite a lot of resistance here to discussing this in any way, people saying keep your head down. But this bank had got to the stage where you can't just keep your head down. His going out and at least being honest – it allowed him to keep his job for another year or so.

At the end of 2013, RBS published a review, which it had commissioned, on its lending patterns. It found when it received the report that, as Desai said,

> *it made quite uncomfortable reading. Basically it said there had been some failings. We had said we would abide by the recommendations – so the new CEO Ross McEwan [appointed a month before the report came out, in October 2013] went out and was interviewed by Robert Peston [then BBC economics editor] and it was tough, but he was upfront, said this shows there have been failings and we'll accept the recommendations.*

In these cases, and many like them, the PR response is due to a mixture of elements – a recognition, as Desai said, that the issue was so high profile and the bank so much in the spotlight since its massive crash and bailout that the bank would be haunted by it; the fact that a leading business paper had pounded away at the bonus story day after day; the very large pickup of the story on social media; and the hope that the BBC's ace inquisitors would, by taking the place of the angry public in the harshness of their questions, lance the boil of rage.

Simon Walker, who has represented a series of big corporations including Reuters and British Airways and now runs the Institute of Directors, believes that Hester was 'an excellent head of RBS' and suffered unjustly – but agrees that the job of PR is 'to get a hold of the scale of the problem', avoid the 'dribble effect' by going out with the truth – but make sure that the person pushed out from behind the rock to take incoming fire is 'someone who seems user friendly'. Walker, when at British Airways, thought his CEO did not have the requisite skills to talk on TV about a fire at Heathrow which caused large inconvenience to passengers – and finally found a former steward, then working the counters, who had the requisite fluency and conviction on the tough break for customers, but also about the difficulties staff face when dealing with thousands of passengers surging about them.

Broadcasters see the tough interview as one of the crowning glories of their trade, and the humbling of politicians and public figures reduced to inarticulacy or refusal to answer are part of their esprit de corps (ironically, the most 'successful' in these stakes was a *Today* programme interview by John Humphrys of the then BBC director general George Entwhistle, woefully underprepared, in November 2012 – which completed a slow-motion destruction begun by a row over child abuse by former presenter Jimmy Savile, prompting Entwhistle's resignation later that day).

Yet if the interviewee is competent, well briefed, and shows the required contrition coupled with a credible determination to change, s/he will usually survive, possibly strengthened. As Desai hints, the hard interview is something of a ritual joust in which both sides must be well armoured. When both interviewer and interviewee know their part in the game – one to probe and emanate scepticism, the other to admit to what cannot be denied and be sincerely sorry – both sides gain.

Above all, when a large mistake is made public, one must be swift and comprehensive. Walker, faced in an earlier incarnation with a large scandal for a client he will not name, thought an interview with the *News of the World* – the revealer of the scandal – would douse the flames. 'It absolutely bloody didn't. Someone said to me after: if you've got a pile of shit at your door you don't take a teaspoon and spoon it into the gutter. You take a shovel and get rid of the whole bloody lot. I learned a lesson from that – though you have to know what constitutes a pile of shit.'

Data drives

Sir Martin Sorrell, head of the conglomerate WPP with several PR companies in its portfolio, told a *Wall Street Journal* breakfast in April 2014 that the PR business had become 'what you know, not who you know'.[3] Sorrell singled out for praise the Penn Schoen Berland research unit within WPP's subsidiary, Burson-Marsteller, which specialises in poll data and has driven the strategy for the agency based on the data it has collected. PR, faster than journalism, is becoming a data-driven trade.

Both PR and journalism have been, to a greater-than-acknowledged extent, seat of the pants enterprises, in which assertions, campaigns, and ideas were only lightly tested if at all. The dramatic story or the slashing column was prized more for its readability and popularity than for its accuracy; in PR, the effect strategies were having could to an extent be measured by the amount of attention they garnered in the news media, but it was at best a rough guide.

Now, the use of data can give much more precise information on the moods and patterns of consumers – who voluntarily and usually unthinkingly transmit to companies the shape of their lives through the transactions they have with shops, banks, their computers, and each other. PR becomes a more precise trade and, in becoming so, claims to offer more added value to its clients. The huge sets of data can, when properly sorted and interrogated, produce a different kind of transparency – that of the customers, whose preferences, moods, and activities are much more visible to the agencies seeking to persuade them.

Grayling's CEO Pete Pedersen stresses the adoption by his company of big data strategies, seeking to attract clients by offering to bring them up to speed on their use of the customer data relevant to them. It launched a series of 'BrainFood' events in the spring of 2014, designed to discuss the issues surrounding data use. In the first of these, the UK's Information and Data Privacy Advisor Richard Thomas argued that

> we've got to get clear market rules about what's on and what's not on. *There are huge benefits to big data – Google says it can track influenza epidemics through searches. The wrong sort of sharing, buying of data, you can get it really wrong. There is no such thing as truly anonymised data [...] When you see billions being spent buying companies, what they're really buying is customer data. There is so much data out there, we ain't seen nothing yet.*

As we'll see in the next chapter, that is much more the case in political communications. And in the US, the success of the data-based work of Ezra Klein, formerly of the *Washington Post*, and Nate Silver, formerly of the *New York Times* – now both working more independently, though still within the protective ambit of a large company – points a new way for elite journalism.

Escaping from journalism

Paradise now

Public relations, from its inception, needed journalism and thus journalists: it had to win their assent, and thus a place in their columns. The mendicant position of PR has long excited the contempt of journalists, who see themselves as able to scorn those who need them more than vice versa: that position is now reversing.

In a description of the recent – past 30 years' – history of public relations, the head of Weber Shandwick in Europe, Colin Byrne, presents the first part of the story as a doleful situation for PR. 'You wrote a press release and hoped journalists would use it. You were totally dependent on the journalist. The communication was all one way.' This is heavily freighted with old grudge, but it expresses something of a truth: what other channel was there to the people but the media? What other way to have a chance of good coverage but to make journalists happy, to put on stunts which attracted their attention and filled their columns, and to establish a line of rewards which might be cut or reduced should coverage be hostile or absent?

That is diminishing. Byrne's second period is one in which PRs were coming to terms with the fledgling internet's possibilities – leading on to the third, the present, in which 'the net moved from a Google operation to one where the clients themselves are proactive, and they create, share and broadcast content which goes direct to the groups they wish to have it'.

This is an influential PR executive's version of a Divine Comedy: Hell, Purgatory, and Paradise. 'Content' – much of which is journalism, or journalism-like material – is now a major theme because public relations professionals see themselves as taking over much of what journalists had thought their own, in every field, from celebrity fluff to political analysis. This reflects the weakness of the media and the growing strength of public relations: and the largest part of both that weakness and that strength has its roots in the internet, which enforces the disintermediation of the gatekeepers who sifted material and determined how it was to be presented.

Few public relations people would say that 'we are the masters [of content] now'; and many, correctly, stress that the mainstream media remain important for them. But the PR executives know that it is more their time, at present, than journalists'. They are also right to observe that, among the millions of messages that come and go in the 'space of flows', in Manuel Castells's (2009) phrase, discrimination between that which is originated after grave discussion in the *New York Times* editorial board and that which comes from an intern in a PR company is less clear than it was, since the journalistic hierarchies making the first important and the second trivial are collapsing. PR is better suited to a free-floating environment, where a 'just fancy that!' piece tied to a personality or a product can fight on equal terms with a weighty announcement.

The large reservation at the heart of this surge of energy is that PR has always worked through 'third-party endorsements', which were generally the news media. A PR-inspired story, or feature, or broadcast news item or programme, was and usually still is worth more than an advertisement. Going direct from corporation to consumer cuts out the middle-hack, and thus is more nakedly self-interested. That is why PR companies now spend much of their time getting other third-party endorsers – like the popular Mumsnet – to recommend or at least mention their clients. Still, a media endorsement, especially from the high-rolling organisations like the global *International New York Times*, *FT*, CNN, BBC or the largely national newspapers, magazines, and broadcasters counts big, especially in the eyes of clients who get their name printed, their face in a photograph, or their voice in an interview.

But there is also a reservation to that reservation. The internet, as well as being a great disintermediator, is a great equaliser, especially when used by younger generations. If Unilever – long a 'media corporation' as well as a consumer one – can put out compelling content, who cares if it is not done by a legacy media organisation? As we will see, the company aims to do just that – and is in the vanguard of the movement of many others.

Journalism becomes content

Colin Byrne was apprenticed to the political communications trade by Peter Mandelson, the former Labour cabinet minister whom he describes as 'the greatest political strategist of his generation, a master of ideas'. In his Holborn, London, office he says that 'when I worked with Mandelson the journalists were the gatekeepers. Peter would say – don't think newspapers, think pictures, think TV. TV was the way of getting round journalists, a group of whom were hostile to Labour and tried to keep a grip on all information.' Unsaid in this is the need for a political party, or any other institution, to feed broadcasters with images and excitement which they increasingly privilege over 'boring' issues like policy.

This early lesson from one whom he credits as his main mentor lays the basis for his present belief, which in differing forms is common within the trade but which he expresses more firmly than most. That is, that PR is now able to create content both for and with its clients which rivals anything journalism can do. 'The idea is that companies won't have to rely on journalists to get their message out. It's part of the change that's happening everywhere. Companies can become, more and more, general interest channels; it's usually a matter of finding out what people are interested in. There's a big interest in learning about brand.'

Byrne and his colleagues had announced, in March 2013, a new content marketing unit called Mediaco,[4] which the company's global head of digital Chris Perry says brings together 'newer, sexier native advertising, to the social side of things'. Perry says clients now want to create a 'compelling content model', and to distribute the content as widely as possible. 'Native advertising' is advertising or sponsored content designed to look as much as possible like editorial or normal programming.

In more speculative vein, Byrne wonders about the future possibility of 'writers in residence': journalists who would be hired by a large company and tasked with using it as their subject, its employees as their sources, and their output pieces about the company which would be as readable (or watchable: much of the output would be video) as anything made for print or broadcast. They would, of course, be under some obvious constraints: but would these be more or less than an average newspaper reporter, constrained by time, space, and the paper's political stance?

Is it PR? Is it journalism? No, it's native!

The idea is not confined to Weber Shandwick, or PR agencies, and it has been some time in coming: it has been 'the year of content' for the past three years, according to one trade watcher – though it may really be in 2014. It has now been taken up, with large investment and enthusiasm, by the *Guardian*, which has created in Guardian Labs a unit which offers corporations its services to produce content to order. A team of (in April 2014) more than 130 will, drawing on the paper's editorial and other strengths, produce content on companies' specification for 'native advertising' while retaining the paper's standards and policies. Native advertising is advertising designed and written to accord as closely as possible with the newspaper's typographical and literary style. The obvious danger for the newspaper and benefit for the advertiser is that readers will not notice the difference and accept the advertisement as part of the newspaper's coverage – and thus the *Guardian* is taking some care that the Labs conform to its image and interests, and the advertising material is clearly labelled. The unit was launched in February 2014 with the announcement that it had signed a £1m-plus contract with Unilever to promote 'sustainability initiatives' – a project which chimes with the interests of Paul Polman, the company's CEO.

The newspaper to which the *Guardian* has become most linked is the *New York Times*, the two working together through joint editorial projects such as the publication of some of the material stolen from the US National Security Agency by its former contractor, Edward Snowden. The *Times* is liberal, like the British paper, if less radically so. In January of this year, the paper's CEO – the former BBC director general Mark Thompson – announced that it would carry native advertising, always marked clearly as advertising material. Like the *Guardian*, the *New York Times* is dedicated to a high-cost, high-quality-journalism model – and in its case, though profitable, is only marginally so: both need the money.

Thus its January announcement,[5] like that of the *Guardian* the following month, was fleshed out by the news that the computer-maker Dell was running a six-figure, three-month campaign using the new format. For that, the company gets a blue box on the right side of the *Times'* web home page which links to the 'paid posts', as the native advertising is called. These posts, which will remain permanently on the *Times'* site and will be discoverable through the search function, sit on a page which is marked as 'Paid for and Posted by Dell'; at the page's foot, another disclaimer – 'This page was produced by the advertising department of the *New York Times* in collaboration with Dell. The news and editorial staffs of the *New York Times* has had no role in its preparation.'

A comment on the Hill + Knowlton website remarked a few days after the announcement that, 'from a business perspective, the lines between PR, marketing, advertising, planning, branding, digital build and now news publication are becoming increasingly blurred ... the key question for media organisations is whether they can claw back the loss of revenue through brand partnerships while preserving editorial integrity.'[6] The adoption of native advertising strategies was said to be an element in the departure of Jill Abramson from her post as executive editor of the *New York Times* in May 2014. Thompson, as CEO, had increasingly assumed charge of video content and native advertising; they were authoritatively said to have warred on this before Abramson was fired in May 2014.[7]

Hacks: still of use, for now

The relationship which was sketched out by Byrne of Weber Shandwick was a hellish vision of the PR executive as supplicant to the haughty journalist. Byrne puts it gratefully in the past: and most in the trade would agree that is at least weakening. But it is not over: lunch is still a medium for persuasion and casual hints calculated to assist clients, and the press still benefits from 'junkets' – especially if they cover one of the burgeoning specialties in the consumer field. Junkets could and still can be anything from a lunch or dinner to a full-blown foreign trip. There is a very funny passage in Michael Frayn's comic novel of Fleet Street, *Towards the End of the Morning* (2005), of a foreign trip for travel writers (or anyone who wanted to go), which ends badly. Most real ones did not, however, and, as Tim Burt (2012) writes, there was an 'unwritten contract' which laid down that good copy should be the result of an enjoyable few days. That is not over.

In a June 2010 piece in the *British Journalism Review*, the journalist turned PR executive turned PR academic Trish Evans writes that a typical foreign student in her class, 'failing to understand the nuanced persuasion of gift bags, drinks or a day at the tennis asks – "Why not just pay them to write the story?".'[8]

Junkets and shows are the PR team's equivalent of the Roman circus: mounted, often at some expense, to get coverage for the product, personality, institution – or cause. In 2000, when she was head of PR for the National Society for the Prevention of Cruelty to Children, Evans put on a gala evening at a big theatre in London's West End to publicise the large scourge of the violence visited on children, often by their parents or others who care for them. Tony Blair, then Prime Minister, Prince Andrew, and other luminaries graced the platform; stars donated their time and talent. It was successful, and by the standards of the day, big. But big now is much bigger.

Junkets are increasingly transformed, and in being so, lose their 'nuanced persuasion' in favour of overawing the journalist so completely that s/he will have no choice but to represent them as they are. This aims to bypass journalists at the same time as putting them in a ringside seat: increasing the spectating experience, but reducing the space in which the reporters can put their own spin – which, most PR executives believe, is much more lethal than anything they themselves can do.

Ed Williams, the head of Edelman in the UK, instances the launch of the latest game from Halo, a multi-billion franchise created by the Bungie video game developer, now owned by Microsoft and tasked with developing games for Microsoft's Xbox console. The game, number four in the Halo series, is a further episode built round an interstellar war between humanity and a theocratic alliance of aliens led by a group of warrior priests named the Prophets. Williams, whose company was one of several involved in the launch, says that 'we were aware it had to be huge – and so we took over Liechtenstein!'

That is only partly hyperbole: the *Daily Mail* wrote: 'for the launch of the Halo 4 game, Xbox claims it is the first firm to ever transform the

Principality of Liechtenstein [population: 35,000] by taking over some of the country's most iconic landmarks, including a 13th century castle and a working mine'.[9]

This launch was a postmodernist creation, calculated to appeal to contemporary sensibilities, its purpose designed not so much to please journalists as to produce content. Williams said that 'we recreated the Halo universe: we invited about 80 journalists, including bloggers and social media, and the effect was huge, with millions of tweets and messages, and coverage on CNN'. The launch was directed by David Fincher, a very successful Hollywood director, who had directed *The Girl with the Dragon Tattoo*, *The Social Network*, and *Fight Club*: and voice-overs were provided by the TV talk show host Conan O'Brien and his on-screen sidekick, the actor Andy Richter. None of these came cheap.

The project marks a break between past and present/future launches on the one hand, and past and present/future journalism on the other. It was designed to be instant: the event, whether a multi-million-dollar extravaganza or the humble, century-old interview, either bypasses the journalist and goes out on channels owned or controlled by the corporation and the PR teams working for it, or it passes quickly through the journalist, who is encouraged to display it across many platforms.

Increasingly, PR agencies refer to the client-mandates as campaigns – even using military metaphors such as 'withstand sieges', 'go over the top', or engage in 'trench warfare' to secure a positive reputation outcome.

Pete Pedersen of Grayling contrasts the set-piece journalistic interview in which the piece is noted down, transcribed, written up, and published – a matter of some days, even weeks – to the modern version, in which the interview is recorded, videoed, put out on social media, and may be tweeted even as it is taking place, producing, cumulatively, hours of content across several different platforms. As in the Halo launch, the creation of the published material has shifted, from the journalist to the agency.

The old-fashioned junket, for all its mild corruption, was in the end in the hands of the journalist to fashion into an article, or a broadcast package: it was a point of honour to be able to trash a junket, even if done rarely, or at least with care. The Halo launch provided much more vivid content than any journalist could match – a gift to social media, which could simply reproduce the images interspersed with awed superlatives: the *Daily Mail* story, replete with dramatic photographs, reads more like a publicity handout than a journalistic narrative.

Halo was an extreme – not so much cancelling journalists out as reducing them to the contemporary version of transcribers. More worrying for the journalist was a piece in *PR Week* in September 2008,[10] in which several respondents to the question 'What has changed in PR in the past quarter century?' instanced the increasing marginalisation of the journalist. Andrew Caesar-Gordon, who runs a media training agency named Electric Airwaves, said that though most young PR executives know little about journalism, 'that doesn't seem to bother them because understanding the processes journalists go through is now a small part of what many of them do'. Deborah Saw, managing director of Citigate Dewe Rogerson Corporate, said that in the 1980s 'newspapers and broadcast were the only way people had to find out what was going on, and all that mattered to us was who was making the programmes and what the editorial agenda was. Now, when I talk to new joiners, they are much more interested in social media.'

Yet most of the colleagues of these PR chiefs are careful to stay onside with men and women who can bite them and their clients hard should they choose to – and since no one will read the coverage as carefully as the client, PRs still spend much of their time making the journalists happy. The St Peter guarding Byrne's Paradise has not shooed the hacks away from its gates yet – though the trend to do so is clear enough. Says Tim Burt of Stockwell: 'PR is now about going direct: journalism was about mediation and is now being circumvented ... the death of what had been PR – that is, it works through journalism – is happening, but happening slowly.'

We give you the numbers

What does public relations still value journalists for? In London, as in New York and Singapore (and to a lesser degree Frankfurt), they are still valuable to financial institutions – especially those from the business press, which can move markets and set, or confirm trends. Vanessa Neill, Director of Corporate Communications in Europe, Middle East, and Africa (EMEA) for Credit Suisse, describes a relationship which sounds almost like a series of tutorials at a business school.

> *Journalists obviously need information from bankers, and equally bankers are very keen to know what journalists are writing about them ... two*

weeks ago we had an emerging markets round table and that was actually for Reuters. We had a number of different bankers across the products and regions talking about the general trends ... through these types of events you are getting to know the journalists really well.

Calvin Mitchell, Vanessa Neill's boss, the Director of Corporate Communications at Credit Suisse in New York, repeats the question:

Journalism down and PR up? Not quite right, baldly put: or at least it's more nuanced. The major brands still have great value – people will read the FT, the Wall Street Journal, they will look at Reuters, Bloomberg and they give them credibility. People will see stories in these journals and will think that the fact they are publishing them lends weight. You can't underestimate that.

Mitchell's endorsement point is shared more generally: newspaper stories carry weight which the millions of commentaries swirling on the internet each day do not – in part through force of tradition and habit, in part because the international brands – *FT, Wall Street Journal, The Economist, International New York Times* – place accuracy as one of their benefits to subscribers.

Mitchell also speaks to a division in the press which is widening: that between the globalised papers and the national ones. All newspapers are now globalised, because all (more or less) are available on the internet. But someone who reads the *Scotsman* in Hong Kong or *Gazeta Wyborcza* in Toronto is likely to be Scottish or Polish, at least in origin: one reading *The Economist* in Lagos is likely to be in business, or in a profession. Among dailies, only the global business papers, plus the *New York Times*, the *Guardian* – 'the world's leading liberal voice' – and the *Daily Mail*, with a website crafted to mix vividly outraged stories with a very long tail of celebrities, scandals, royals, and 'Just Fancy That!'s are in the league of global newspapers, benefiting, of course, from being written in the world's lingua franca. Ruby Quince, Creative Digital Director at Freud Communications, says that 'The *Daily Mail* is international, because it deals with celebrities and they are now an international currency. The *Mail* has seen the new media world most clearly.'

Ed Williams of Edelman says:

I think there's a barbell pattern in the mainstream media. At one end there's the big global media – FT, Wall Street, Economist, NYT, BBC,

CNN; at the other end the specialist magazines, like Foreign Affairs, New Yorker. In the middle there are many, many publications whose guts have been ripped out or are being so – that includes big national papers all over the place.

Implicit in both Mitchell's and Neill's descriptions is an assumption of common interest. As Neill says, 'journalists obviously need information'; as Mitchell says, the international 'major brands still have great value'. Both sides find value in each other, since both can gain from the other.

Yet the relatively staid style of the business press is changing – one reason why Neill and Mitchell pay such close attention to their representatives. At Goldman Sachs, the Director of Communications Jake Siewert says:

This is a crude analogy, but I say that business journalism turned around the time of Enron in 2001 and Tyco in 2002 [both companies had been lauded by the press and then collapsed, with their chief executives – Dennis Kozlowski at Tyco and Jeffrey Skilling at Enron – convicted of fraud and sentenced to lengthy spells in prison]. Till then business stories were mainly about business leaders and the journalists were encouraged to get close to the CEOs as much as possible, and they were perceived pretty much as heroes – like Jack Welch [former head of General Electric] and Sandy Weill [formerly head of Citigroup]. But then along came Tyco and Enron and they were like Vietnam and Watergate – it's imperfect as a parallel but there's something to it. Business journalists are close to political journalists now, looking for scandal and malfeasance – that's what tends to land on the front pages.

If Siewert is right, then it increases the pressure on PR executives to keep journalists close. David Shriver, managing partner of Tulchan Communications, sees the increased investigative side to financial journalism as, in the end, helpful.

I see the business press still fulfilling its role pretty well. For a company now it's about taking a 360-degree view. There are only a few places in the world where the nexus between capital and media take place, and that's New York, Singapore and London. London has deep pools of capital and a very inquisitive media – and that's useful because it means people take their business seriously.

We give you the words, and everything

A journalist working for a PR company is nothing new: most of the early PR executives had some experience in journalism, and that has continued. It is different now largely due to the content creation demands and the need for PR professionals to think like journalists.

Employing former journalists enables PR companies to produce copy that can be used quickly and easily both online and in print format. Phil Hall is the founder and boss of PHA Media, which works from a crowded office in Soho: he was also, in 1995–2000, editor of the *News of the World*, then editor in chief of *Hello* magazine. Much of his business is in the celebrity area – though he also represents companies, especially those active in entertainment.

Hall told us that much tabloid 'reporting' was public relations-generated material. It was not, as Neill said, just about 'making it easier for journalists'; rather, it is making it *so* easy for them that the PR does almost everything.

> *If you look at a national newspaper, anything up to 50% of the content will come from a PR company, whereas about 10 years ago, it would have been only about 10%.*
>
> *The sources for stories are now the PR companies because the PR companies are inhabited right across the board with former journalists, whereas previously there were very few and it was generally PR executives. There were enough jobs in journalism to keep journalists employed but there aren't now and there are more and more journalists in PR. PRs are the gatekeepers of news and information but they are also now becoming the sources: stories are being led by PR companies and PR companies are inhabited by journalists.*
>
> *The large redundancies at newspapers have led to the more corporate supply of content and PR going directly to output. PR teams are emailing copy around and focusing on the key parts of the story. Journalists run with the amended version because they're understaffed and rushed. PR-controlled copy means it's running with more facts correct, as the PRs don't make as many errors as the journalists. The PR teams do supporting research as well.*

In Hall's telling, the hollowing out of newspaper newsrooms has meant that, in tabloids concerned most of all with celebrity, the journalists' contribution to the finished newspaper can be minimal. Celebrity PR still needs journalism – or its appearance: it needs journalists (beyond those who work for the PR company) less and less.

James Thomlinson, head of Bell Pottinger Wired, says:

> *Ex-journalists have a nose for a story. They can pick out the key facts that will make good headlines. They can also analyse information and present it in a concise form and help sell it into newspapers. Not only do we look for print journalists to employ, but with the prolific growth in video content, strong broadcast journalists are also playing an important role in PR strategies. We are seeing the two industries merge.*

Many press releases, in particular those geared towards female lifestyle, fashion, and beauty, are now written as news items. Press releases where PR companies have provided the content, the storyline, and the images in order to make the pitch as convenient as possible are common. This is most prevalent in consumer PR, where press releases often appear similar to a page from a magazine: such press releases are packaged so that they can be run word-for-word.

The corridors of influence

With the grown-ups

From the earliest days of PR, some of its pioneers became very large and influential – both Edward Bernays and Ivy Lee made excellent livings and were much courted. Today, the bosses of the big companies, now often conglomerates uniting advertising with PR firms and more – such as Maurice Lévy, since 2013 joint CEO of Publicis; John Wren, head of Omnicom (these two failed to merge as this was written); Sir Martin Sorrell, head of the WPP media group – have long been very large global players; as has Richard Edelman, head of the biggest independent PR agency in the world. These are Davos men, whose wisdom on how the world of business, or even the world in general, is going, is sought and reflected on. Now, the heads and senior directors of the PR companies which are part of their empires are increasingly large figures.

PR executives say they are being drawn in deeper and deeper to the core business of the client. The CEO of a large London agency instanced work for a multinational and famed engineering company, for which it had once done largely financial PR based around its quarterly earnings statements and annual report and results:

> We continue to do the financial media for them, engaging with the financial reporters, engaging too with investors to make sure their investment case is known and understood. But suddenly the company is interested in a much broader range of issues – under the present leadership, they've decided they want to have a debate round the role of value added in manufacturing in the UK economy, the need to rebalance away from an over reliance on financial services – so suddenly you're making an essentially political case to a political audience. You're, yes, mindful of media reaction – but you've also got politicians, the labour movement, NGOs – suddenly you're part of a debate about what the British economy is going to do and you find yourself having to rebuild a consensus around the need to rebalance the economy. It's a much broader job, broader constituencies.

Because the constituencies are more numerous and varied, and because what the company or the agency addresses to them is invariably accessible either in real time or stored information, the narrative has to be consistent. David Shriver of Tulchan says:

> prior to Deepwater Horizon [the rig in the Gulf of Mexico, leased to BP, which exploded in April 2010 killing 11 crew and leaving the well drilled into the seabed gushing oil] BP was calling itself Beyond Petroleum. They had had an analysts' day three or four weeks before the incident, everyone had a huge number of slides and only one of these was on the future – and it was beyond the horizon. Mostly they were saying, we're better than others at getting oil out of the ground. So what was driving their thinking? Was it that? Or Beyond Petroleum? That kind of misalignment is now immediately obvious.

The alignment of goals, says Shriver, speaks to transparency and its outcome – the need for truth.

Tim Burt, in his *Dark Art*, says of his 'art' that 'professionalism is in: the party atmosphere is over'. At Finsbury, Roland Rudd – named the most influential PR executive in London by *PR Week* in 2012 – says that the question of status *goes back to the relationship with the CEO and the chairman. High stakes. You must be on the top table: you need that dialogue ... earlier, we were always called in to advise, but now, often, you get much more leeway. We have been advising Verizon on their buy-out of Vodafone in the US: we've been involved in talking about it for a while. In a way, communications almost comes first, finding out how the market will react, how we get ourselves in the best possible position.*

In the spring of 2014, Rudd's Finsbury was advising AstraZeneca, Brunswick advising Pfizer, in a merger deal which did not make it: the public battle was as much between the rival PR strategies as between the two pharma companies' offers and industrial plans.

At Portland, CEO Tim Allan says that one large client – whom he would not name – had retained the firm to advise on a relaunch after the new CEO decided that the company had become 'toxic' to the public – 'Now that's really interesting, high grade work, complex and absorbing. You need really good people for that: we now employ people with first-class degrees from Oxbridge.'

The conversation

All companies are media companies: the phrase is now a clichéd trope in PR circles, but it has real and growing force. It is a product, once more, of the internet: the company now creates packages of narratives, from the simple 'this is who we are and what we do and why we're good at it' through to sophisticated, multi-million-dollar projects aimed at inserting the company into a number of different environments – financial, political, social, NGO-created, even philosophical – with a large presence and strong content of its own.

Ruby Quince, Creative Digital Director at Freud Communications (its creator, Matthew Freud, is, like Bernays, a relative of Sigmund: in his case, a great-grandson), woos companies – sometimes shy and reluctant – into a digital world where they are at least potentially 'online all the time'. He believes that

we're getting to the point where social media aren't a way of just ticking the box: clients are moving towards using social media at the core of their

business. They realise that people are finding them through social media
– and see that monitoring what the social media are saying about them is
very important.

My clients had thought that their online presence was under their
control. But the social web isn't under their control. They are beginning to
understand that there is an ebb and flow of different kinds of content. PR
work is now focused on reputation ... we want clients to consider their
reputation as a strategic part of their image.

BP, still reeling from the oil spill disaster of 2010 and facing possibly more huge fines in US hearings early in 2015, has abandoned 'Beyond Petroleum' and is spending $500m in North America to improve its image, emphasising efficiency rather than environmental concern and using its own staff as a fund of stories about 'brilliant minds' who are striving to solve the world's energy problems.

It licensed one of its PR professionals – who became known as 'Arturo of BP' – to engage with the Wikipedia website, identifying himself openly and editing material on BP on the site. This has given rise to a debate between 'Arturo', the Wikipedia editors, others involved in the BP campaign, and interested readers, over the rights and wrongs of an employee, and a public relations executive to boot, editing his own company's material.

In effect, 'Arturo' engaged in a running series of debates with the Wikipedia editors and other contributors, each arguing the case for his version and, in Arturo's view, usually coming to a compromise. The debates spoke to Quince's observation (above) that monitoring comments on a company is crucially important – especially on Wikipedia, since the site has become the source of information most commonly referred to when one wishes to check up on a company or an individual, and thus bears directly on reputation.

In the 'conversation with the public' stakes, one company usually comes up among PR executives – Unilever; and one person – Paul Polman, its CEO for the past five years. The CEO of a large London agency, an admirer of Polman, says that

he has said that if you can bring down the Egyptian administration in
six days of the Arab spring, think what you do with Unilever! There's a
sense of fragility everywhere after the crisis; and if you talk to Polman,
he also feels there's a real sense of transparency and he is subject to the
wishes of a mass audience in a way never seen before. The conversation

has changed, I think: after the depression, it's almost as though it's not PR any more. It's about – is this real? Because if it's not, you'll be found out.

Social responsibility renewed

Polman, with some other CEOs, has taken part in a series of 'Conversations with global leaders',[11] in his case conducted a few months after he took over at Unilever in 2009. A significant part of the conversation – an interview with Adam Bird, a McKinsey director – allowed Polman to boost his company through linking the reduced spending power millions of people were experiencing with products designed with tighter budgets, and more stay-at-home meals and evenings, in mind.

But he also sought to promote Unilever as a company which focuses on nutrition, hygiene, and water – both because they are areas in which Unilever has products or which affect the business, and because he believes the company can assist by reducing energy use relative to its output. Asked by Bird what concrete steps he was taking, he said that

> *at the end of the day, our brands need to grow, but we think it's very important that our brands have what we call 'the social mission'. Ben and Jerry's is a good example of that – a key fighter against climate change and nuclear weapons ... the consumers' trust in business is, unfortunately, lower than we would like it to be. And the standards that the consumer sets – the expectations, her own proactiveness and influencing with her purchase decisions and her own beliefs, are only going to increase ... so companies with a strong social mission will be companies that are more successful long term.*

Polman has retained and deepened this social mission, hosting a 'Nutrition for Growth' summit to address global malnutrition in June 2013, a week before a G10 meeting in Northern Ireland, bringing together the UK Prime Minister David Cameron with his opposite numbers from Tanzania, Uganda, and Malawi, with other chief executives and scientists. But he has also had the giant company develop a web-based channel called 'The Adrenalist', which features short, exciting videos on such 'extreme' sports as hang gliding, rock climbing, and marathon running (Polman is himself a marathon runner, for charity).

The channel's home page says, fairly discreetly, that it is 'powered by Degree' – an anti-perspirant marketed under that name in North America, as Sure in the UK and Ireland, and Rexona in most other countries. The CEO of one of the agencies Unilever uses, who did not wish to be named, said that 'Unilever is the biggest spender on marketing in the world – it's identified a core group of buyers, young men, 20–35, heavily invested in sports, especially high-adrenalin sports – it's put out files and files of videos on this; it's a good example of a company becoming a media company.'

The shift, according to several PR leaders, is away from a strategy which demonstrated that corporations did good things – an approach known as Corporate Social Responsibility (CSR) – to one affirming that what the company is doing is itself good, or at least essential. Polman, of course, does both – able to do so because he has many hundreds of brands, some of which can lend themselves to promoting socially responsible causes.

At the 2014 World Economic Forum in Davos, Richard Edelman argued that business leaders now had the responsibility to ascend the 'bully pulpit' and argue their case – whatever it might be – in public, moving into areas which had once been shunned for being 'too political' but now were essential because the business of a company was not any longer merely business, but the effect it has within, on its employees and suppliers, and without, on the environment, on its neighbours, on its customers. This move was backed by the findings on Edelman's annual 'Trust Barometer' which showed in early 2014 that corporations had recovered some of the trust lost in the previous few years, but politics and government had not. Public relations now sees itself, and markets itself, as a skilled mediator for its clients of the burgeoning networks of influence, of demand and supply, and of political and social change.

It is an argument for the public relations function, now much more broadly defined than ever before, to be as close to the right hand of the CEO as to the chief financial officer, or operating officer, or technology officer – and to point him or her out into the world. The CEO, Edelman believes, should, as well as its original meaning, also stand for 'chief engagement officer'.

Doing good

Ethics for engagement

Ethics in PR, as in much journalism, is often regarded – even (at times most of all) by those working in these trades – as a contradiction in terms, the two unable to coexist except hypocritically. Yet there is no doubt that, among PR professionals, there is now an attempt, at different degrees of intensity, to insist that ethics are now more present than they have ever been. The most organised expression of this within the profession which we discovered was in the formation, in late 2013, of Jericho Chambers in London, a company which marketed itself explicitly, even aggressively, as a centre of advanced ethical behaviour. Its two founding members were Robert Phillips, formerly head of EMEA at Edelman, based in London, and George Pitcher, a co-founder of the PR company Luther Pendragon in 1992, a former journalist and an ordained Anglican priest. Phillips is the new firm's CEO, Pitcher its chairman.

Pitcher has for over a decade believed that 'spin' is dead (even as operators like Damian McBride were proving it could work very well, at least in the short term). In his *Death of Spin* (2002) Pitcher argued that 'communication comes from principles'. On the eve of establishing Jericho Chambers, he said that the

> PR industry approach has been based on the belief that you could manipulate reality – and that's over now. Companies are becoming aware that they're accountable to a much larger public constituency than ever before.
>
> The essential thing for public relations to do is to help companies make the connection with what they do rather than what they say. You need to change corporate behaviour. Banks, for example, have to move from a merely compliance culture to a values culture. The old CSR model – we're good really because we encourage our staff to volunteer – that's gone.

Robert Phillips, with Jules Peck, another ex-Edelman executive and a former adviser on sustainable development to the Conservative Party, started Citizen Renaissance,[12] a web-based centre for debate, led mainly by Phillips and circling round the need for 'more citizen-centric thinking and an end to the global imbalance of wants and needs'. It is partly and admittedly utopian, partly practical, infused with the belief that – as Phillips wrote in September 2012 – 'a new class of citizen influencers is emerging, challenging the dominance of those moribund elites but not yet fully "bottom up" in nature'.

Applying this to the PR trade in another post a month later, Phillips wrote that

> communication professionals today must [...] connect and immerse themselves with both Deep Science and Deep Humanity, they must be both mathematician and storyteller; architect and philosopher; able to find as much commonality with the Chief Technology Officer as with the Chief Communications Officer or the CEO [...] in this Age of Engagement, where we have the ability to connect deep science and deep humanity, businesses must re-focus on societal factors that will restore, build and retain citizen trust.

In an interview, Phillips said that the modern CEO must be the 'chief activist' among a network of activists, rather than a smooth counsellor.

In a conversation at the Ivy Club, a favoured spot for PR leaders, Phillips said that 'public relations isn't dead, but it is no longer fit for purpose – it has an obsession with outputs rather than outcomes', leaving the trade at the mercy of marginalisation. Further, PR had not grasped the importance of data in establishing more scientifically based relationships; ignores structural issues in the rush to communicate something, anything; and pushes ideas which are 'tactical' rather than transforming.

Phillips says these ideas are becoming more widespread: he instances Pierre Goad, co-head of communications for the HSBC Bank from 2011. In a post on the bank's website, Goad wrote:

> We don't waste our time crafting the perfect message and most efficient channel to plant communications in people's heads. Implanting messages doesn't work with 5-year-olds let alone with 259,000 grown-ups. Instead we set out to create a more transparent environment to support our business strategy.
>
> We wanted to help people listen to each other [...] work is a profoundly social experience. Large organisations do everything in their power to deny that. We limit the ability to interact yet what we have come to appreciate is that communication has to be in every direction. Valuable information is missed if the manager on the walkie-talkie is permanently

> *pressing the Talk button. Exchange is not primarily a feedback mechanism.*
> *It does not need to lead to action. Rather it creates a safe place to*
> *communicate in an unstructured way.*[13]

Phillips, who in his gap between leaving Edelman and founding Jericho Partners has read widely, also credits Cliff Oswick, Professor of Organisation Theory at the Cass Business School at City University in London, with insights such as 'control is futile'; 'all types of leadership are redundant'. He credits Miguel Pestana, Unilever's Vice President of Global External Affairs, with an ability to marry promotion of the company with an active campaign for sustainability.

These leaders rummage widely for ideas among people still seen by many of their peers as dangerously anti-business: Oswick did an interview with the famed linguistic pioneer, writer, and anarchist Noam Chomsky on what use business schools could be to society; Phillips sees the role of the CEO as no longer to lead, but to disrupt. Their strategies are only now, in the mid-2010s, being applied.

Love me, love my soap

The one campaign to which Phillips does give some (qualified) approval is the Dove (soap and other beauty products) campaign for real beauty – a campaign which ran, first of all in the UK, in 2004 and featured women of differing ages and races, including women who were in their seventies or eighties, overweight and of average looks – accompanied by such slogans as 'Wrinkled? Or wonderful?' The campaign was in part based on polling which showed that only 2% of women considered themselves beautiful.

A video was produced, which had a number of women come to a studio and describe their faces to a police identikit artist who sketched them without looking at them from their description of themselves: then did another sketch from another woman's description of them. The exercise displayed the uncertainties and nagging self-criticisms the women – mainly young or young-middle-aged – had about their looks, with an anxious search for crows' feet and pallor. The revelation of the two sketches to the women by the artist showed that the self-described renderings were always less attractive than those described by another – leading many of the women to say that they should be more aware of the beauty they had rather than that they aspired to; several cried on camera.

The campaign was a mix of advertising (by Ogilvy & Mather) and PR (by Edelman, and Harbinger Communications of Canada). The fact that the video went viral – more than 62 million views on YouTube – and that the debate about its ethical probity hummed along for months on the internet, meant that the leverage gained by Dove and its parent company, Unilever, was estimated to have augmented the campaign by thirty times. It was a novelty, yet at the same time harked back to the beginnings of PR in uniting women's issues with a product. Edward Bernays staged a 'Torches of Freedom' march in which young women joined the Easter Parade in New York in 1929, smoking cigarettes – linking the then strongly running trend for more social emancipation for women with a boost for the cigarette companies.

The Dove campaign did not treat its women customers as fools who reached for a product marketed under at least implicitly false pretences; it sought to give the dignity of ascribed beauty to every age, race, and body shape. It did not, though, reach into structural or 'transformational' issues: an overweight woman of colour with many children in a Colombian favela was unlikely to be reassured by – assuming she saw – the campaign, or by any of the Dove products. It demonstrated the limits to what could be done while remaining within commercial logic – that is, continuing to sell more product, as Polman said was essential to the company and his future at the head of it.

The darker part of the art

At the other end of the scale is what is seen as *un*ethical behaviour – most commonly thought of as that PR which puts itself at the service of individuals and regimes which have bad records on criminality, or human rights. The issue is hot in London: (Lord) Mark Malloch Brown, chairman of EMEA for FTI Consulting, says he is particularly concerned by it because London, as one of the two or three major financial centres of the world, is the target for companies and individuals seeking respectability and endorsement of some kind from its institutions.

> *I think the issue of taking on countries and individuals who are very dodgy is now a real problem ... in Africa one is seeing land and energy deals done which are not by the book, and then being brought to London where expensive bankers and lawyers clean up the deal. I think it's a real*

problem, not just for PRs who are asked to represent the people involved
- it's the whole industry which surrounds this.

Malloch Brown – who came into PR via political consultancy, mainly abroad – became deeply involved in one such imbroglio. FTI represented an Israeli entrepreneur named Bernie Steinmetz, reputed to be Israel's richest man with a fortune of $9bn, who had received a contract from a previous President of Guinea, now dead, to develop what is said to be a fabulously large and valuable store of iron ore in Guinea, one of the poorest countries in the world. The present president, Alpha Condé, tried to get out of the contract – believing Steinmetz, about whom many negative stories circulate, should not develop the deposits – but could not.

Steinmetz hired FTI to represent him in Guinea and in one version,[14] FTI spread negative stories about the President and his son, Alpha Mohammed Condé. However, an FTI executive who came to oversee African accounts protested against the Steinmetz contract: Malloch Brown terminated the contract in 2013, to the fury of Steinmetz, who sued him, alleging that Malloch Brown had told colleagues that he would not work for a murderer and a crook (the case was settled out of court, with neither side admitting fault). Malloch Brown is a close friend of the billionaire philanthropist George Soros, who supported President Condé and the NGOs in Guinea who were working against Steinmetz. Steinmetz became convinced that the philanthropist had conspired with the former UN Deputy Secretary General to destabilise his business. Malloch Brown said that Soros warned him against Steinmetz, but dismisses any conspiracy.

This is poignant, for Malloch Brown is one of the sharpest critics within the industry of public relations representing shady characters and institutions. 'PR professionals give themselves an easy way out when they say that it's the same case as everyone having a right to a lawyer. There is indeed a requirement to make the best case you can to a client – but not to engage in falsehoods and misrepresentation.' He has also been critical of the man whom many in the PR business see as the largest problem in this area, a fellow member of the House of Lords, Tim (Lord) Bell.

Several leading PR people agree with Malloch Brown that London's reputation as a laundry is dangerous for it. Richard Edelman, in New York, said:

There are some real practitioners of the dark arts. Public affairs (which includes representing governments) is only 10–15% of the revenue of PR.

> *Yet image wise – 'Wag the Dog' [a reference to a 1997 film of that name, which showed a PR man arranging a war with Albania to cover up a presidential affair] is definitely the image.*

In *Dark Art*, Tim Burt comments that 'London may come to regret its image as the world's largest PR launderette'.

Anne Gregory, Professor of Public Relations at Leeds Metropolitan University and a long-time campaigner for higher standards in the industry, chairs the board of the Global Alliance for public relations and communications management – a body which, at its meeting in Melbourne in 2012 with 800 delegates from 29 countries, agreed the 'Melbourne Mandate', committing members to 'define an organisation's character and values', 'build a culture of listening and engagement' and 'instil societal, organisational, individual and professional responsibility'.

In the last of these commitments, PR professionals are enjoined to 'demonstrate societal responsibility by creating and maintaining transparent – open, honest and accessible – processes and credible communication that balance public interests with organisational needs'. Gregory says that

> *PR has been an enormous force for good in society, giving a voice to the voiceless and power to the powerless – its low esteem is due to those who abuse the trust placed in them, who do things like burying bad news on the day the planes hit the World Trade Center [as a Labour Party press officer, Jo Moore, said she did in an email]. We need to grasp the nettle of ethics if we are to gain credibility and long-term respect.'*

The public relations trade's grappling with ethics has been mirrored, in the UK, by that of the press. The UK's tabloids, the most powerful popular newspaper press in the world in its hold on a national audience (though now declining) and its influence on society and politics, were found to be, in differing degrees, indulging in hacking into mobile phones, harassing and blackmailing sources, printing manifest untruths, and paying bribes. The original revelations – mainly by Nick Davies in the *Guardian* – of phone hacking at the *News of the World* (the UK's most popular paper, owned by News International, the then UK arm of News Corporation, subsequently closed) were followed by more revelations in subsequent years, and by the evidence submitted to an inquiry set up by the government and chaired, from 2011, by Lord Justice Leveson.

The response of the UK press has been varied: the first reaction was sackcloth and ashes, especially on the part of Rupert Murdoch, founder and head of News Corporation – a period which prompted the closure of the 168-year-old *News of the World*. Later, in leaked remarks he made to members of the staff of *The Sun*,[15] the daily tabloid now the UK's most popular paper, who were angered by the provision to the police by the company of large amounts of data on its employees, Murdoch said that he had 'panicked' and 'perhaps gone too far' and that the company was now fighting to keep information from the police. Most newspapers now attack Leveson and the government for what is variously described as attempts at censorship and 'Stalinism'. The largest part (by circulation) of the UK press has shown itself to be more ethically compromised than public relations. It has vowed to change, and set up a new mediator with regulatory powers, called IPSO; others, who favour some kind of state backing, profess scepticism that behaviour will, in the long run, change.

The royals

Word was out – perhaps put out by one of the Palace servants who adds to his or her income by informing newspapers of royal titbits – that one of the Queen's corgis had died. The reason why this was very big news for popular papers tells much about why they are popular. The royal family has long been and remains a site of widespread imagining, and to dismiss it as a monarchical soap opera is too snobbish: it has some soapy features, but it is much more exciting in being really unpredictable. So – given that the Queen does seem to be fond of corgis, having demonstrably so many of them – it would be a large addition to pleasurable public imagining and to conversations to know the depth of her grief over this one's passing.

Thus a corgi, in death, could be the star in a story on the front page on which, in life, it could only have appeared as an extra in a photograph. The royal correspondent of *The Sun* at the time called, in some excitement, to the duty Palace pressman, and asked for the Queen's reaction to this. It was late in the evening; the pressman was doubtful that the Queen would respond to a request for an emotional response on a dog's death at any time, and certainly not at this. He refused to ask. The reporter insisted, asking finally – how would you feel if your dog died? Well, said the pressman, I guess I'd feel pretty upset. The reporter rang off: in that unguarded comment he had his story – 'Palace insiders say the Queen was distraught' was the basis of the next morning's banner headline.

This story, told off the record like much else of Palace life, speaks to a culture of mutual manipulation between news media and public relations at the very apex of British public life. It is, says a former press aide, 'a symbiotic relationship. The press created them, created the status.' The royal PR team, working with the Queen's advisers and household, and at times with the Prime Minister's office, has the task of projecting the public face of a royal family whose power is at once splendid and empty. Empty, that is, of executive authority, which is held to proceed from the people through their elected representatives and elected government; but full of splendid significance as the constantly displayed capstone of British sovereignty.

Serving at the people's pleasure

Since it is so constantly displayed, it must be popular: the Duke of Edinburgh once remarked that the royals existed in their magnificence only so long as the British people wished them to. It was a media theme, immediately after Diana's death, that their popularity had sunk dangerously low because the Queen remained in her castle of Balmoral in Scotland, did not order the flag flying over Buckingham Palace lowered, and did not give evidence of grief.

This may have been overdone, the reflection of a transient public mood; but the misalignment between the aristocratic reserve (and, possibly, not too much grief) on the one hand and the apparent need of millions to bear witness to an astonishing devotion was evident enough, and provided the main dramatic tension in the 2006 Helen Mirren vehicle, *The Queen*. It was held to be one of Tony Blair's most savvy acts, prompted by his director of communications Alastair Campbell, to come out in public a few hours after her death with a short, apparently heartfelt tribute, in which he invoked her as 'the people's Princess'.

Campbell, who had many years as a popular newspaper journalist between his government job and his Cambridge degree, had understood the extent of popular, especially female, affection for Diana, and saw the opening for linking that to the still-new New Labour government – which had been less than four months in office. Diana, after all, epitomised one who stood up to established, old-fashioned power just as New Labour had in overthrowing an 18-year Tory governing hegemony; she was socially liberal; supported good causes, such as mine clearance and the fight against AIDS.

It is a delicate task, to project dignity and popularity – though one made easier by the huge dependence of the media on the Palace communicators: 'the relationship was hard to handle but always predictable', says the former press aide. The PR aides must be careful to guard their treasure but must also know how precious it is to press and public, and how difficult the transition will be from the popular Queen, with more than 60 years as the royal standard, to the long-delayed assumption of the throne by Charles III. He has gone through periods of real unpopularity, especially with women, because of his slighting of, and unfaithfulness to, Diana. That has seemed to wash away, though it may return.

The Sun wot shunned it

An account of some of the tensions which seethe in the royal entourage was gained in an interview which Mark Bolland gave to the journalist Mary Riddell for the *British Journalism Review* in 2004. Bolland had been Charles's press aide, 1996–2002, then was retained as a consultant. Soon after leaving the staff, a rumour surfaced – heard by Sir Michael Peat, Charles's private secretary – to the effect that a Murdoch tabloid was trying to get a lock of Prince Harry's hair in order to run a DNA test.

> *Michael told me that a distinguished lawyer had told him about the story. [He] told the police and talked to lots of people before talking to the newspaper. He didn't involve me because my friendship with Rebekah [Wade, now Brooks, then editor of The Sun] was seen as something wicked, and Michael wanted to handle it himself ... the trouble with telling the police is that news leaks out. Rebekah made it very plain she was very cross. She was adamant that the story wasn't true.*

Charles III, as he will be if and when he becomes king, may be difficult to manage into a sympathetic image. The former press aide said that the Prince

> *could never understand why the fact that a valet put paste on his brush in the evenings was such a negative image. They could never get it – didn't*

understand what I was going on about [in projecting a more demotic sensibility]. He had to give a urine sample and a poor valet had to hold the bottle!

His mother had photographs of her and her sister Margaret in the wartime uniforms of the Auxiliary Territorial Service, in which Elizabeth was a mechanic and truck driver. Charles's photographs of himself at the same age would be from the elite Scottish Gordonstoun boarding school, and at polo – both tough proving grounds, but not popular.

The Queen, save for the charge that she showed too little public emotion over Diana's death, has been off limits for criticism. Charles, who has been much bloodied by tabloids and has been shown to loathe them, cannot expect such treatment. The coming revolution in British royal PR will be a test case for the trade, the toughest test that British public relations, which prides itself on being toughened in the furnace of an aggressive press, is likely to face.

In sum

- Internet-prompted transparency, and the more open and decent behaviour it is held to encourage, is a large element in the way in which PRs now present themselves, though transparency can only be a force for change where the institution or individual fears, or has suffered from, widespread exposure.
- Ethical behaviour, always a contested area in PR as in journalism, is now a more central issue; as is the fear that some London agencies depend too much on commissions from clients with dubious reputations, and thus give the industry a negative image.
- The internet and social media allow public relations agencies and in-house teams to put out material directly to stakeholders, customers, and the public at large. More and more companies and institutions are becoming 'media companies'. But the third-party endorsement given by the media remains precious, and journalists are still sought after.
- The need for a rapid and comprehensive apology by the most senior executive in a company is an increasingly necessary part of a PR's armoury; a harsh broadcast interview is valued for clearing the air and 'moving on'.

- The use of large amounts of data, both to define PR priorities and measure outcomes, is being rapidly adopted by the trade.
- The status of public relations within the company, and in successful agencies, is growing, with more communication directors approaching or joining the board, and heads of agencies directing the public profile of companies undertaking large projects – such as a merger – or in crisis.
- Corporations may continue to have programmes of Corporate Social Responsibility, but the trend is to regard these as add-ons, where the more successful strategy is to emphasise the social and other utility of the client's core business, and to construct platforms for company leaders to participate – judiciously – in wider social and economic debates.
- The British royal family is at the apex of UK public relations – at once the most prestigious and the most delicate of exercises in presentation and in supporting an image, and of global significance. Nationally, the handling of the transition to Charles III, and the bolstering of the popularity of his reign, will be central to the continuing cohesion of the UK. In Queen Elizabeth II, public relations has an invaluable asset; the test will come when she relinquishes the crown.

3

Political Communications

The trade of political communications has suffered from the same atmosphere of contempt which much journalism visits on politics – heightened by living behind the scenes, and thus becoming more suspect. A British book on special advisers, whose job includes managing public relations for the ministers they serve, was titled 'People who live in the dark' (Blick 2004). The process is known everywhere as 'spin'.

Political communication is now much more central to politics than it was in the past. Its role is at once more pervasive and less sinister than is commonly believed. More pervasive, because polls, focus groups, testing of policy messages are now highly professionalised and the techniques increasingly globalised, and the more effective for political leaders when least noticed by their publics.

Less sinister, because the communication techniques have not rendered all policy-making and government activism wholly dependent on them: policies and governance continue to be based on strong beliefs by politicians on what the political process can bring to citizens. It may or may not be true that, as a recent work on 'reinventing the state' puts it, 'the west is losing confidence in how it is governed' (Micklethwait and Wooldridge 2014). But it has not lost the capacity for political belief or action.

Set out here are what seem to be the most salient developments in contemporary political communication – taking the examples mainly from the US. That is because there is so much more of it in that country, and the very large funds applied to developing it make it the undisputed world leader in the trade. The US spend on political communication is far ahead of most other countries, and it is assumed to set the world standard. In spring 2014, David Axelrod, a former senior adviser to President Obama, became senior strategic adviser to the Labour Party leader, Ed Miliband.

The heritage

Machiavelli as spin doctor

James Harding, former editor of *The Times* and from early 2013 head of current affairs at the BBC (a large and skilful user of public relations advice), writes of 'the sense [in the political world] that real power lies today in the hands of the political consultant, the modern Machiavelli' (2008).

Machiavelli's name, and the strategies he proposed for rulers, are often coupled with the PR executive or the political consultant. Machiavelli recommended, as a matter of course when deemed necessary, deceit and subterfuge to the modern prince. But he is more important for what public relations claims to have become.

Maurizio Viroli – who takes a strongly divergent view (2014) of the Florentine from the pejorative one which has been popular since the sixteenth century – writes of Machiavelli: 'for him political reality was made of many elements: passions, powers, interests, intentions, ability to simulate and dissimulate [...] a world of uncertain and ambivalent signs, words and gestures [...] the true realist, the true leader, is a person who is able to imagine grand ideals, and to work, with prudence, to make them real'.

This is the way in which the most successful of public relations and political communications practitioners now view themselves, and in which some have always seen themselves. That is, they see themselves in the mould of Viroli's Machiavelli, as *consigliore* to leaders in all walks of public life; as advisers who accurately interpret present and future reality, who push the prince (or client) to accept reality and to proclaim the truth, and who can thus best position their clients, the modern princes, for success. The bedrock skill of the political consultant is to interpret for his political client the reality to which he must address himself: to have 'grand ideals' but to 'make them real'.

Modern political communications

Several large changes were behind the appearance and growth of modern political communications, around the turn of the nineteenth and twentieth centuries in the United States, which in turn caused large shifts in the economy and in political life. Political parties, set for decline in the latter part of the twentieth century, were in the late nineteenth century becoming increasingly important, at the federal, the state, and the city level; they were machines for advancement, for the acquisition of power, for reform, and for graft. The power they wielded and the discipline they required both grew greatly, especially in the period between near the end of the nineteenth and the first two decades of the twentieth century, when progressive politics – then largely the preserve of the Republican Party – came to the fore, and the state and its agencies became more proactive and intrusive in the commercial world.

Both the state and the parties required public relations advice, on which they have continued to depend in the succeeding decades. Now, the party is thought by many political PR people to be in terminal decline, in part because it has been replaced by them.

The US presidency became more activist

As the US presidency became more oriented towards change driven from the top it needed persuasion more than before: the same was true of other political leaders. The (Teddy) Roosevelt presidency in the first years of the twentieth century made a pact (Goodwin 2013) with the leading journalists of the day – aimed at having them identify, and even map out, the economic and social reforms required. They were investigative reporters, but were also believers in the benign nature of government and the state. Early public relations shared much of that belief in the state's efficiency and beneficence, a belief which depended in part on the state being a client.

Journalism was also becoming more activist

The journalists on whom Roosevelt depended were largely clustered around *McClure's Weekly*, whose founder and editor, Samuel McClure, argued that 'the vitality of democracy' depends on 'popular knowledge of complex questions'. Newspapers were much less high-minded, but they too began exposés of the seamier side of city life, and would at times inveigh against the trusts and support the 'little man'. The investigative tradition, which *McClure's* did most to embed into American journalism, waxed and waned in succeeding decades, but it was generally stronger and more respected than in other countries until the last decades of the twentieth century, when it became more widely diffused.

The greater proactivity of the press in business and political affairs made the case that both needed more PR protection. The US economy was booming, rapidly creating an urban working class and increasingly dominated by ever-larger corporations – such as Standard Oil, Union Pacific railroad, US Steel, and JP Morgan. These companies increasingly became major players in the economy and thus, inevitably, in political life; in the progressive era, beset as they saw it by government, trade unions, and journalists, they began to seek protection from public relations that they charged to give their side of the story. As Edward Bernays put it, 'public relations is the name business gives itself when it recognizes itself as a political entity' (2011). After the Great Depression of the late 1920s, the same case for the necessity of PR to re-establish trust in capitalism was made; it was made again in the late 2000s, after the financial crash of 2008.

The party hollowed out, political communication fills the space

The gap between the high ideals and often higher promises of politics on the one hand, and the reality of winning and keeping political power on the other, is a space increasingly filled by political communication. As in other forms of public relations examined here, it is growing in power, influence, and resources: the stakes and the rewards are generally higher, and the media which must be served are more voracious, more numerous, and most importantly more varied, the differing modes of communication demanding different tailorings of the messages.

That space *had* been largely filled by political parties; they were, and to a very diminished degree still are, the sites where enthusiasm, partisanship, loyalty, and at certain times hard electoral work could be organised and debated. From the latter years of the twentieth century to the present day, however, they have answered to fewer and fewer needs of a politics organised with and round the media. For the most influential analyst of the contemporary party system, the late Peter Mair, the failings of the parties to address a supercharged media-ised political world means that 'the age of party democracy has passed [...] they no longer seem capable of sustaining democracy in its present form [...] what we see now emerging is a notion of democracy that is being steadily stripped of its popular component – easing away from the demos' (2013).

The leading political consultants interviewed are or were, in all cases, politically committed as well as in politics for a living; they see themselves as an increasingly essential addition to the political world, tasked with rousing voters' enthusiasm for candidates through the media. They now adopt new techniques which they admit can carry disturbing implications for democratic politics, but which may also revive public participation through the use of the new digital technologies, especially social media.

The inflating price of democracy

The constitutional commitment to free speech in the US has been interpreted to mean that limits on spending on electioneering should be minimal: in the last few years, these limits have largely been legislated away. In 2010, the US Supreme Court struck down limits on independent campaign spending by corporations and trades unions; in April 2014, the court struck down 'a decades-old cap on the total amount any individual can contribute to federal candidates in a two-year election cycle. The ruling, issued near the start of a campaign season, will very likely increase the role money plays in American politics.'[1]

Money played a huge amount in the 2012 presidential election. Both candidates – the incumbent Barack Obama and the challenger Mitt Romney – spent more than $1bn,[2] the first time the billion dollar limit for campaign spending by one individual had been breached. Most of this goes to television – though, as we will see, an increasing amount is spent on social media, an area where Obama has been especially strong. It is also the area where Romney fell victim, as a waiter at a private fundraiser he attended in September 2012 took a surreptitious video on his mobile phone of the candidate claiming that 47% of the American public are 'dependent on government', 'believe that they are victims', and 'believe the government has a responsibility to care for them' – then tweeted the occasion with the video attached.

This kind of expenditure is foreign to European states – though not elsewhere: estimations from the election in India which brought Narendra Modi to power in May 2014 put his spend, funded by corporations eager for his business-friendly policies, at least £500m.[3] It is also high (relative to national income) in Japan and several Latin American countries. Campaign spending in the UK is strictly regulated and (by US standards) very small: parties cannot buy TV time, but are given free time for election broadcasts. They are limited to £30,000 ($50,000) per candidate, coming to almost £20m ($33.5m) if all constituencies are fought.

The more regulated and therefore more modest the campaigns, the less razzmatazz – and corruption (at least of any size) – is likely. Britain, which has one of the raunchiest and most scandalous popular newspaper cultures in the world, is puritanically mean about expenditure on election campaigns; the US, with newspapers of (usually) high ethical and professional principles, likes to let the campaigns, and their financiers, rip. Thus political PR, which began in its modern form in the US, remains rooted in its political soil and draws its innovations, imaginative, and technological, from there.

The Lie Factory

The first company which had political consulting as its core business called itself Campaigns Inc., and was founded in California by two former newspaper people, Clem Whitaker and Leone Baxter. Jill Lepore writes[4] that, like all Californian Republicans (the party held virtually all the state-wide offices), they were horrified by the prospect of the socialist writer, Upton Sinclair, winning the gubernatorial election in 1934. And so they put into operation a strategy for beating Sinclair which would seem to justify his name for them: 'the Lie Factory'.

They scoured Sinclair's many books for quotations which would make him look foolish, or sinister, or in some way un-American. They ran an ad in the *Los Angeles Times* headlined 'Sinclair on marriage', with the line underneath – 'The sanctity of marriage … I have had such a belief … I have it no longer'. But it was not Sinclair's belief about marriage: after divorcing his first wife on the grounds of her adultery, he married his second wife and remained married to her for nearly 50 years, until her death a little before his own. The quotation was from one of his novels, the 1911 *Love's Pilgrimage*. As Baxter said later, when it did not matter, 'Sure, these quotations were irrelevant. But we had one objective: to keep him from becoming governor.'

The couple were writing a template for a new trade. It included injunctions like 'woo voters'; 'make it personal'; 'attack the opposition' (if there isn't one, invent one and attack it); 'claim to be the Voice of the People'; 'see subtlety as your enemy'; 'Simplify simplify simplify'; 'Never shy away from controversy'; 'win the controversy'; 'Put on a show!' Jill Lepore writes that 'no single development has altered the workings of American democracy in the last century as much as political consulting' – a very large claim.

But it has considerable justification. Whitaker and Baxter's Campaigns Inc. set the tone by proclaiming ruthlessness. Later political communicators could eschew and some did eschew the hard-boiled cynicism and amoral policies of Baxter and Whitaker: but they could never ignore the fact that their techniques, when applied with skill, usually worked.

Lee Atwater

Lee Atwater is the man who, far from ignoring Whitaker and Baxter's lessons, widened and deepened their take-no-prisoners mould. The Georgia-born Republican communications operative rose to become, uniquely for a political communicator, Republican Party chairman. Atwater was a creative and hyper-energetic man, who updated and sharpened the Campaigns Inc. model, and in doing so became the man to emulate by both his followers and his opponents. In a 1989 profile the writer Eric Alterman quotes the Democratic congresswoman Patricia Schroeder as saying that 'the real problem with Lee Atwater is that his tactics are contagious. Can you beat Lee Atwater unless you join him? ... [He] did not start the campaign consultancy business but he may be the man most responsible for the way it is practiced today.'[5]

In his critical biography of Atwater, John Brady (1997) shows both his innovative talent and his ruthlessness. He eschewed press conferences, seeing them as 'risky pseudo events'. His dirty tricks became legend: he said of one opponent that he 'didn't accept Christ as his saviour' (he was Jewish); on another occasion, he broadcast the story that a Democratic nominee for Congress, Tom Turnipseed, had been 'hooked up to jumper cables' as an adolescent – that is, had been treated for depression by electroshock. That was true, but as Turnipseed later wrote, Atwater boasted of his initiative to many journalists, and seemed 'to delight in making fun of a suicidal 16-year-old who was treated for depression with electric shock treatments' (Brady 1997).

Atwater was the beneficiary of the aftermath of Watergate: before, aides had been relatively modest, known about by the press but not regarded as decisive to a candidate's winning or losing. After, writes Brady, there began

> *a journalistic game of 'gotcha' that turned reporting into flank attacks. Candidates needed more protection. Thus was born a new breed of hired*

gun, consultants who brought a specialized knowledge of today's enormous communications network and sensitivity to the perversities of human nature. They ran polls, conducted focus groups and created a candidate's image, they manipulated the press and invented news ... (1997)

The successful presidential campaign he ran in 1988 for the then vice president George H. W. Bush featured what is still the most famed negative TV spot – centred on Willie Horton, a black convict serving a life sentence for murder who, after having been granted a weekend parole which he broke, committed assault and rape before being recaptured. The furlough programme under which he was granted temporary parole had not been initiated but had been extended by Dukakis. An ad featuring Horton was run by a group supportive of the Bush campaign; one produced by the campaign did not show Horton, but used the controversy over the parole and showed sinister-looking men moving in and out of prison. The ad, which attracted charges of racism, is believed to have played a major role in Bush's victory, as Atwater, his campaigns manager, pounded on the Horton theme relentlessly.

Atwater's tactics are not copied everywhere, and there are more constraints on those who wish to emulate him. But his negative campaigning, and his spreading of damaging rumours, remain a stock-in-trade of many.

Reading the society

The communications tyro's nastiness is better attested – because it could be so shocking – than his strategic canniness, but Atwater had both. Never an intellectual, he still had the journalist's talent for jackdawing useful wheezes from big ideas writers. In the mid-1980s, one of the biggest of these ideas was Alvin Toffler's *The Third Wave,* which argued that, after the first two waves of agriculture and industrialisation, there came the information society – which Atwater adapted to political use by arguing, in a memo for George H. W. Bush, then the vice president preparing his own presidential campaign, that this meant a growing mass of people who were 'anti' in outlook, anti-Big Government, anti-Big Business, anti-Big Labour'.

This 'anti-' group could be enticed into either political camp if a strategy could be crafted which combined both continuity and change. It was a shrewd assessment of a new mood: Bush did win the presidency, running against the Democratic Massachusetts governor, Michael Dukakis. Atwater was given high honours in the party he served so diligently for all of his short working life, in part because he won by any means, but also because he was an astute reader of social trends – a dispassionate skill which all successful political consultants must develop.

Personality politics

The personality politics which emerged in the US in the 1950s and elsewhere in the next decades was, of course, not the first time politicians were presented as personalities: democrats and dictators alike knew well the imperative to delight, cow, or in some way impress themselves on the people. But before the age of political communications, the personality of the leader who had risen to the top of the heap, either through the party or through revolution/coup or both, was more or less a given, which was not seen as open to change except by his own decision.

The main democratic leaders who rearranged a large part of the world at Versailles after the First World War – US President Woodrow Wilson, UK Prime Minister Lloyd George and French Premier Georges Clémenceau – were aware of the usefulness of the press (especially Lloyd George), but did not submit to being groomed by public relations; nor did the men – Joseph Stalin, Adolf Hitler and Benito Mussolini – who were preparing for dictatorial power in the Soviet Union, German and Italy.

After the 1960s, political communications professionals argued that this was no longer possible, even in authoritarian states. Thus leaders who had, or wished to have, good relations with the Western powers and who felt the need of support in unfamiliar election campaigns turned to the individuals or companies willing to work for them. This was of course a commercial relationship – and the fees could be very high. But the relationship was usually attended with a dash, or more than a dash, of concern for the deepening of democratic practices and norms.

In his book on Sawyer Miller, the pioneer among US political consultants working in developing states, James Harding wrote of the company's early forays into Latin American elections, noting that 'David Sawyer spoke no Spanish [but …] he did not need the local language to understand a political conversation that, to an American, took such a familiar shape […] the [political] dialogue was being transformed by television' (Harding 2008). TV was the universal language – not, for the consultants, its content, which was of course in Spanish, but its power over the viewers, especially inexperienced viewers.

Sawyer Miller, and the consultants who followed the trail they had blazed, believed an election was an election was an election, and that to dominate the election the candidate had to dominate television. They had some success, especially in Venezuela: but the man who was to rule the country from 1999 to 2013 did not want 'Yanqui imperialists' as his advisers, and knew very well how to dominate through television. Hugo Chávez did not understand what his economy required, and in his long presidency drove it to near ruin, which impacted most of all on the mass of poor people whom he had wished to help. But he understood how to act on the Venezuelan stage, and on the Venezuelan screen.

The extreme personalism which Chávez demonstrated was hard to emulate – few leaders would want to talk for eight hours, as he did in many of his TV appearances – but it has served as a kind of authoritarian template, on which Vladimir Putin of Russia, using the state-directed TV channels, has rung changes, as images of him in various poses and characters are broadcast at intervals and his public appearances and speeches, even when routine, are always prominently featured. Putin does have a changing team of image makers – all Russians, highly unorthodox by established PR standards (see below) – but takes from Chávez the need to be always dominant.

Getting the message right wins

A non-American who took a leading position at Sawyer Miller was the former *Economist* journalist Mark (Lord) Malloch Brown, later a senior official in the United Nations, later still a Foreign Office Minister in the Labour administration headed by Gordon Brown (2008–10), now head of the European office of the consultancy firm FTI. He says that the firm learned much from working in developing countries, which it later applied to corporate work.

> *Sawyer Miller's concept of strategic communications was the idea that the power of the correct message could overwhelm everything in its way. Sawyer would say that even if the other guys were outspending you by*

10–1, even if they had a whole government machine behind them and
your clients were a bunch of dissidents with photocopiers – if you got the
right message you could overcome all of that.

Scott Miller, in particular, became convinced that business was a field of
politics, that CEOs were political candidates, and that 'every voter [was] a
consumer, every consumer a voter [...] politicians and products were
much the same' (Harding 2008). The large common denominator was
emotion: the right message was not so much a popular policy as a popular
image, or the candidate's own personality.

Inherited models

Political communication inherited a set of models and examples, from
corporate PR and other influences, practices which have been more or less
followed until the present, some of which are now said to be changing.
These practices included the following:

- A habit of ruthlessness: the election result has been king, and because
  the outcome is much clearer – '50% plus one' – its achievement or
  failure to achieve is far more climactic, and can make or break
  politicians and their consultants more quickly and sometimes finally
  than the less easily measurable success or failure in corporate work.
- A drive to keep it simple: this was based on the view, still current, that
  the average voter is uninterested in politics. Clem Whitaker of
  Whitaker and Baxter said that 'a wall goes up when you try to make
  Mr and Mrs Average America work or think'. Few, till the present day,
  demurred from that insight; now, internet-based interactivity has
  elevated the voter from the status of an easily programmed dummy
  into a much-courted actor.
- An emphasis on emotions, much more useful in political campaigning
  than reason: candidates had to be fitted to an admired stereotype,
  opponents to one which was threatening. An early choice must be
  made between presenting the candidate as status quo – thus the
  need to emphasise mature wisdom and the judgement of experience
  – or change, calling for qualities of radical impatience with the
  present state of the country and a driving desire to reform it root
  and branch.

Joe Napolitan, born in Massachusetts the son of indigent Italian immigrants, and a former newspaper reporter, was the first individual (as distinct from a company) to hawk his political communications skills round the world. He was clear that what was needed was not facts, but emotion. Relating an argument he had with the advertising company DBB over a spot for the Democratic presidential candidate in 1968, Hubert Humphrey, which he believed too replete with facts, he wrote that 'I thought we should aim for warm, emotional messages in our television spots', and argued for commercials 'which take the viewer on an inner trip and utilize information subconsciously stored in his mind. Triggering responses from stored material is [...] more effective than giving the viewer a mass of new material to learn (because learning is one of the most difficult of the brain's jobs ...)' – an endorsement of Whitaker and Baxter's 'Simplify Simplify Simplify'. TV spots, and the campaign as a whole, had to be designed to release emotional responses and attitudes already buried in the subconscious (not for nothing was the man who stands at the beginning of the trade a nephew of Freud's).

A much studied endorsement of the appeal to the emotions came from one who combines psychiatry with political consultancy, Dr Drew Westen (2007). Westen instances the campaign TV ad which a young Bill Clinton ran in his presidential campaign in 1992, beginning 'I was born in a little town called Hope' and continuing with a mention of his father's death a little before he was born, his boyhood handshake with President Kennedy and 'I remember just, uh, thinking what an incredible country this was', and his using the idealism triggered by the meeting to go back to Arkansas after his education, when 'I didn't care about making a lot of money, I just wanted to go home and see if I could make a difference'.

Westen wrote that Clinton narrated the ad's commentary with 'exquisitely moving emotion', making it 'one of the most effective television commercials in the history of American politics'. The 'political brain', writes Westen, is not a desiccated calculator of political advantage; it is an emotional hothouse, where evocative images and music and a simple, powerful narrative do most of the work. 'Reason is the slave to emotion', he writes, crediting David Hume with the insight, and chiding Democrats for 'clinging tenaciously' to 'an irrational emotional commitment to rationality'.

To continue now with the practices favoured by political communications:

- A recourse, especially when behind in the polls, to negative campaigning, while much derided, is also much utilised by professionals. Whitaker and Baxter destroyed Lincoln Steffens's chances in California by a series of outright lies; Lee Atwater sank Michael Dukakis's bid for the presidency by taking a legitimate issue on the use of furloughs for those convicted of violent crimes and turned it into an all-embracing smear which played on white fears of black violence. More recently, Karl Rove, the former aide to George W. Bush, has been accused of slipping slurs and damaging rumours into public discussion, notably about Hillary Clinton's mental state.

- A steady conviction that the candidate is always the story; the consultant never is. Famously, Alastair Campbell in the UK became the highest-profile political communications director (to then Prime Minister Tony Blair) in the world – and left early, believing his fame compromised his office. This discretion is especially true when working abroad – since an American or British 'spin doctor' gives ammunition to the challenger (unless the challenger is also using such people). Political communications people know well that they have a bad image, and have usually sought modesty – but not always. Napolitan took on the pejorative image directly – writing, as the first paragraph of his 'how to do it' book, *The Election Game* (1972) – 'I am a political consultant. My business is helping elect candidates to high office. I don't see anything particularly sinister about that, but some people do.'

- A realisation that the candidate is – contrary to early and easy optimism on the part of some consultants – not endlessly malleable, hence you must find his or her strengths and do what you can to disguise the weaknesses. The Weber Shandwick UK and EMEA boss Colin Byrne said – in a slightly testy response to a badly phrased question which suggested that politicians in their first election were more 'plastic', i.e. open to suggestions of change, than experienced leaders – that 'It's not right to say that we produce plastic people. Mrs Thatcher wasn't plastic – what the Saatchis and Tim Bell did for her was to smooth the rougher edges, and work on the hair, the voice, the presentation.'

- A concentration on keeping the candidate clear on the strategy. Napolitan wrote: 'decide what you want the voter to feel or how you want him to react; decide what you must do to make him react the way you want; do it'. Since 'candidates are often unclear in their own minds precisely what it is they want to say to voters, the consultant must insist on this, the first necessity for a successful campaign: decide what you are' (Napolitan 1972).

Journalism dumbs down, and up

Political communication is changing because political journalism is changing; its citadels of excellence now trembling, collapsing, even disappearing. One of the privileged sites from which to survey what is happening is Politico, the Washington-based paper and website, which does what its name suggests: it aspires to be the closest watcher and holder to account of the most powerful complex of governing institutions in the world.

John Harris, one of its two founders, came into journalism in 1985. His was a blessed entry: only days after graduating from Carleton College, a highly rated private liberal arts university, he was accepted as an intern at the *Washington Post* – and went on, some 20 years later, to become its National Politics Editor, top of the political journalism heap in the US.

Yet within a few years, he was planning an exit. With Jim VandeHei, the *Post*'s White House correspondent, he left the paper and founded – across the river, in an office tucked behind a TV station's offices – Politico, with the explicit mission to cover US politics more closely, even more intimately, than a newspaper could or did.

> We thought the old order was crumbling. I came into the business in 1985 – for some years after that I thought, everyone thought, that what was on the front page of the New York Times or the Post was by definition important. By virtue of their sources, ability to promote, the writers.
>
> Then there was a kind of 'Holy shit! What is this about, this new world?' moment. We thought – we don't want to be at the old party any more, we want to be at a new party. Our strategy back seven years ago was to create a niche – that the future is more robust with a niche model than a general one. You don't come to Politico for sports or for news on Afghanistan or whatever … and I'm not saying that I as a journalist find that appealing or desirable – I grew up in the old world, I didn't have any complaint with the old world, it just had to change.
>
> I did cover politics for most of my career but I was doing so in a newsroom with a very illustrious tradition that covered the world. I liked the fact that I worked for a paper that did cover the world. But the

old world is now deconstructed – and it's deconstructed along specialties. Politico's is not going to work unless we cover politics better than the Washington Post.

Auteurs and wunderkinds

At the time we spoke, Ezra Klein, who had since 2009 written Wonkblog at the *Post*, was in ultimately unsuccessful negotiations for the paper to put $10m into Wonkblog to greatly expand it. The paper – which by that time had a new owner, Jeff Bezos, founder and owner of Amazon – refused, and Klein left to go to Vox Media, which did make the investment. His belief, which has acquired the status of a mission, is that people do not have enough information to allow them to judge political and economic issues properly, a deficit which Wonkblog set out to rectify, with well and clearly written backgrounders on current issues.

He has set himself a harder task at Vox. Citing research by the Yale law professor Daniel Kahan, he wrote in an April 2014 essay, 'How Politics Makes us Stupid',[6] that even if people seem to be looking for objective information, they unconsciously select that which backs up their case – a tic that seems to lie too deep for correction. However, there is an antidote. He says that once people realise that policies fashioned for areas which touch them – tax, health insurance – have been based on bad evidence, they will force the politicians to 'face a reckoning at the polls'. Klein, at 30, is a prominent example of what Morris at Politico now sees as the new trend in journalism: the journalist as brand, occupying a unique position, catering to a niche audience who really want to read him. 'Everything,' says Morris, 'old and new, is reorganising itself round individuals rather than an institution.'

As Klein was preparing to leave, the media commentator Michael Wolff noted[7] that the trend for individual branding was quickening among well-known journalists – such as Kara Swisher and Walter Mossberg of AllThingsD, a techy blog; Glen Greenwald, formerly of the *Guardian*, who left to set up an investigative website, 'The Intercept', financed by the eBay founder Pierre Omidyar; Nate Silver of the *New York Times*, who uses large data sets to call elections with great accuracy and left to start the 5.38 blog, financed by the sports channel ESPN; and Andrew Sullivan, among the pioneers of what Wolff called the 'auteur school of journalism', who set up his own blog, The Dish.

After Wolff wrote, Bill Keller, former editor of the *New York Times*, started the Marshall Project, a team of 20 to 25 reporters brought together to write about the US justice system, which Keller believes is failing citizens badly. Though a big name is fronting these blogs, they all employ several people, and thus need a steady income – and/or a generous investor, who may also have to be patient. 'Is there', Wolff asked, 'plausible economic logic to individual journalistic fiefdoms?'

If the answer to the question is yes, this will become and remain a significant part of the new news-media ecology, and it points to a raising of the quality stakes. All of these brands – from the radical investigator Greenwald to the liberal-conservative Sullivan – built a reputation on being nobody's fool. The kind of political journalism which Morris and VandeHei left did much this-is-what-they-say-happened reporting, and was silent about issues which reporters knew or thought they knew but could not verify or did not have the time to fully investigate (one reason for starting Politico). The new brand journalism probes deeper into particular issues, leaving the many, freely accessed general news sites to take the load of filling in the details – something easily done with a blog's hyperlinks.

In this they share a common space with non-journalists who have expertise in particular areas and are often dissatisfied with the coverage their specialism gets. A prominent example is the SCOTUS blog (Supreme Court of the US), started and maintained since 2002 by lawyers, and husband and wife, Tom Goldstein and Amy Howe, who believed that the scale of the importance of the Supreme Court's judgments was not properly reflected in quotidian reporting, nor were the nuances brought out. Writing in 2010, they said that the site gets 15,000 regular readers, with 40,000 coming when a large issue was before the court and up to 100,000 on 'truly huge' days.[8] They also revealed that it cost $200,000 a term (from October to the following June or early July) to run: it is sponsored by Bloomberg Law. The level of seriousness and dedication in Goldstein and Howe's blog is obviously very high, and sets a high bar: but it is a bar other specialists may feel inspired to reach.

Political communicators still pay a lot more attention to the current political writers of the *New York Times* than to ex-*New York Times* writer Nate Silver. But Silver and his comrades in wonk journalism will be a larger part of the future, and are likely – if they are successful, as Silver was in predicting election outcomes when at the *Times* – to be powerful arbiters of the political scene.

A gentler, brighter time, back then

The trades of political communication, together with corporate and celebrity PR and journalism itself, are all experiencing wrenching change. PR of all kinds is coming through it better than journalism, because it retains a business model – in fact, several business models, depending on which sector it works in – and is expanding its reach and competence. But most of the practitioners with some years of the trade behind them experience a loss, and a certain fear or disgust, for the new, as do journalists.

These consultants work with smart journalists, highly competitive and aggressive in their reporting, but the rapid decline in sales and advertising has put large pressures on US newspapers, where editors now order their reporters to be briefer, more dramatic, and less concerned with boring policy and other detail, pushing them to tell the political story through conflict and personality. At the same time, the rise of strongly partisan journalism, especially on radio and television, has leeched audiences away from objective reporting, and rewarded sensation. Thomas E. Patterson, a Harvard Professor of Government and the Press, writes that, in successive Pew Center surveys, journalists themselves revealed their belief that their reporting had become 'shallower', 'increasingly sloppy', and 'too timid' – and that 'bottom line pressure is hurting journalism' (2013). The smart people, in short, are being forced to be dumber, at least in many newspapers.

And not just dumber, but also at once more aggressive and less experienced. Morris at Politico says:

> I do notice a kind of ferocity and an intensity which wasn't there before. It makes it unpleasant. I covered the White House in the Clinton years – Mike McCurry was there as press secretary – we'd scream at each other and tell each other to fuck off – maybe half a dozen times a year, and we both thought it was a big deal. But with the Obama crowd – you might have half a dozen a week! It was like – that's just the way you do it.

Less experience might appeal to cynical political consultants, who could relish palming off an unfounded story on a novice; but on the testimony of Kevin Madden, who was communications director for Mitt Romney when he was Massachusetts Governor and CEO of Bain Capital, inexperience is more trouble than it's worth.

The papers have pulled back their reach. You can see it at the level of people who cover campaigns now – such as in 2012. It's not that they haven't worked on a presidential campaign any more – it's that they haven't worked on any campaign.

They didn't have any of the institutional knowledge you need when you're covering states' races – and because of the speed with which these things are done, you need endurance, so they go for young people. And given the way it's changed, a lot of good smart journalists don't see it as the best place to be to cover the race, they realise that there is this dumbing down, a Twitterisation of the news, that they want no part of – it's not what they find interesting, it's not what they think will inform the wider electorate.

On the other side of the political–consultant divide, Mike McCurry, Bill Clinton's press spokesman in the White House, says, 'When I get on my hobby horse I say that the new trends have dumbed down political discourse because they have made everything sharper – angrier, more designed to elicit an emotional response.' Joe Klein, one of the most prominent political writers of the past 30 years, rides his hobby horse harder: his *Politics Lost* (2007) is a mourning for a politics and a political coverage now gone, an exploration of a world in which politics had become bland and protected at every turn, in every phrase, by consultants – while newspaper and magazine political journalism declined, and broadcasting was captured by partisan shouting matches and stunts shaped for it. His listing of the reasons why, as he puts it, 'the inanity of post-modern public life has caused many Americans to lose the habit of citizenship' include the encouragement by Richard Nixon of a new breed of political consultant, who helped him win the 1968 presidential election – among which number was a young Roger Ailes, the creator of Fox News, whom Nixon made his executive producer for television. Ailes said after the election that 'this is it. This is how they'll be elected for evermore; the next guys up will have to be performers.'

The pushing of senior politicians into the entertainment zone would seem to bear Ailes out. The most intellectually fastidious of presidents, Barack Obama puts himself on to chat and comedy shows, with every sign of enjoyment. In March 2014 he traded mock insults with the actor Zach Galifianakis on his spoof interview show, *Between Two Ferns*.[9] Commenting on the show, the President's chief communications strategist said that 'we have to find ways to break through. This is essentially an extension of the code we have been trying to crack for seven years now.' Mike McCurry, quoted in the same article,[10] was more hesitant, saying that 'we have to worry about the dignity of the presidency, there's a limit about how much you can do' – adding, however, that 'the shifts in the popular culture and the way people are entertained and get information almost mandate new strategies'.

What's in it for Obama? He used the appearances to plug the signature piece of domestic policy – Obamacare: in Galifianakis's show, the comedian sighed deeply when the President first mentioned it, then said wearily – 'OK, let's get this over with', then sat looking bored as Obama plugged the new system, saying at one point – 'Is this what is meant by *drones*?'

Joe Klein and the journalism scholar Jay Rosen – whose Pressthink blog is a long-running and thoughtful regular commentary on the news media – lament a time when political commentary was less diluted by a kind of amoral relativism than they believe it is now: the subject of an August 2012 Rosen essay.[11] He wrote, 'We still need to know who's misleading us more, because our choices are binary [i.e., in a two-party system]. If political reporters can't tell us that [...] then why do we need them?' The claim here is that, in the past quarter century when the press as we knew it started to decline, political journalists lost the memory of why they were performing their trade – since the core of it was gone. The 'whatever' world of the political spinners had infected the spun.

The gatekeepers' clearances

The testimony of the present and former political consultants to whom we spoke is that, though they and others may mourn elements of the past, the field on which political strategies will be deployed will see the emergence of a quite different kind of political communications. To use a metaphor, it will be replacement of toll roads by clear highways, where the tolls are the news media who had commanded the communications between the politicians and the people, and made sure it was conducted on their terms, and the clear highways are made possible by the internet and by social media, where politicians can mix freely with their electors, and the electors can convey, individually or in greater or smaller groups, their views, desires, and complaints to the politicians, unvetted. It is seen as win–win – both politicians and people empowered.

Jake Siewert, now of Goldman Sachs, worked in various posts in the Clinton administrations and was briefly press secretary for four months, 2000/2001.

> *What I think happened was this. In the early 1990s, when I began in the White House, the only people who had access to real-time information were editors, and the people who ran TV stations. They might have a TV feed on their desk, and the wire service – and they had a crucial role in deciding whose voices were heard.*
>
> *You could not be a serious person unless you passed muster with the CBS evening news or the New York Times editorial board ... because they would decide whether your voice, anyone's voice, was worthy of being heard. You could not be a marginal politician – like Ron Paul today in the US – and get attention, because he's an 8% politician. Even by the late 1990s, you didn't have all that they have now, no smart phones, even BlackBerries were for sending emails.*
>
> *But now, if you're sitting at your desk, you feel that everyone has access to information because it's all around ... anyone that has a smartphone and lives in Yorkshire or Iowa – it doesn't really matter – they don't have to be sitting at a desk in the nation's capital. That's eroded hugely the power of the editors.*

His predecessor as Clinton Press Secretary, adviser to John Kerry in his failed presidential bid in 2004, Joe Lockhart, says:

> *a lot of things now seen as news would not have been seen as news before because there were no channels for the content. If the Washington Post and the New York Times and Walter Cronkite of CBS News didn't think it was news, there was no way for you to find out. Now the new technologies allow all of us to become our own journalists.*

Clearing the decks for a new era

A new era tends to be founded on the bones of an old era. This new era of political communications will be marked by the perceived ending of a number of features in both journalism and political communications, some of which are centuries old, many of which will not be much missed, but some of which will be seen to pass with varying degrees of regret.

The end of objectivity

Lockhart was press secretary to the leading democrats Walter Mondale, Michael Dukakis, and Paul Simon – the last of whom tried and failed to gain the Democratic presidential nomination in 1988 – then became managing director of the consulting firm Glover Park Group and later spokesman for Facebook; he is famed for his aggressive defence of Clinton during and after the Lewinsky scandal. Though he has been quoted as thinking journalism 'shallow' – he was a journalist for six years before becoming a consultant – he nevertheless believes that the technologies which allow everyone to be a journalist have a large downside:

> *Now everything is fair game. First the rise of cable news then the net then Twitter have incentivized journalists not to be a Times or a Post man but be their own brand. And when you've got thousands of people out there trying to push their own opinions and be their own brand, then the truth is certainly the first casualty but any kind of objectivity has just gone out of the window.*
>
> *It's true that the Post is still fairly objective, its got very good journalists there … but it used to be that if you were on page one of the Post and you were taken down, often for good reason, then you were done. Now it doesn't have that power. The Times is the remaining beacon of institutional media power.*

His successor has a story which contains in it both the promise and the pitfalls of citizens acquiring – as quickly as buying a smartphone – the status of journalist, even Important Journalist. Says Siewert:

> *This was a great exchange, it involved Michael Hayden, the former head of the National Security Agency. Hayden was giving an interview [in October 2013] to a Time reporter called Mario Calabresi on a train – it was old-school journalism, on background, chatting about the current state of affairs on surveillance. A guy sitting across the corridor can hear this, and starts tweeting it. The conversation ends when Hayden's office calls and says he's being tweeted.*

So he walks over to the guy and offers him an interview – and the guy says, 'I'm not a journalist.' And Hayden says, 'Everyone's a journalist.' I use this story to remind people of that: everyone's a journalist now.

The tweeter, Tom Mazzie – himself something of a political operative; he had worked for the liberal site MoveOn.org – later claimed that Hayden had given 'disparaging quotes' about the Obama administration, and had 'bragged about rendition and black sites'.[12] Still, he had his photograph taken with Hayden, both smiling amiably.

Kevin Madden agrees about the lower standards of objectivity, but his improving tale, set during the Romney campaign in 2012, illuminates how these standards have also become more lax among the press. He instanced a young reporter, 'six months out of J-school', who had learned what she believed was a scoop – that Romney had publicly mocked the former Republican Speaker of Congress and candidate for the 2012 presidential nomination, Newt Gingrich, over something 'heartfelt' which Gingrich had said about his mother.

It was 100% inaccurate, but she put it out on Twitter and it was retweeted everywhere. It really was a case of a lie travelling halfway round the world before the truth could put its boots on. We spent all night fixing an error by someone just out of college, on a presidential campaign. It shows what happens when the premium is put on speed and being first.

Objectivity is one of the battlegrounds of journalism and this is not the place for another exchange of fire. Some prestigious news organisations – the BBC, the *New York Times*, the *FT*, the *Wall Street Journal* – believe both in the possibility of objectivity and its practice. Others – as in the Italian press – deny both. A middle way is championed by *The Economist*: opinionated in its reporting, but careful to present all points of view fairly. In that tradition, Andrew Sullivan's blog, The Dish, has as its motto 'Biased and Balanced'.

The end of automatic respect for the press

Successive presidents have usually hated the press, either throughout their presidency or for parts, usually the last part, of it. The famed photograph of just-re-elected President Truman holding, in November 1948, the copy of the *Chicago Tribune* with 'Dewey [the Republican challenger] defeats Truman' in a banner headline all across the front page shows a usually dour politician grinning with obviously genuine delight: here was *Schadenfreude* able to show itself.

More recently, Bill Clinton, whose unconfined sexuality brought the press to his door, including to the doors of the White House, several times, tried to bypass the press in his first term: Jake Siewert says:

> we used to talk in the Clinton era about going round the mainstream media – at that time we were actually doing regional TV and media, we talked a big game on that. Regional TV was almost always more interested in substance than in who's up and who's down, they were less snarky and always very happy to have the President on their TV. So we'd do these satellite tours ... the regional strategy worked to some extent, it worked best when not overstated.
>
> The national press hated it – that's why it didn't work, they punished you. If you'd just done it and not alienated them – but in the early Clinton days there was a strong message – we don't need you.

It was too early for such a message. Clinton's republican successor, George W. Bush, had a wary respect for the news media's power, but not for their trade. At a rare event put on for the press early in his presidency at his Texas ranch, he mentioned that he did not read the papers much, except for sports. A reporter asked him, 'How do you know what the public thinks?' Bush answered, 'You're making a huge assumption – that you represent what the public thinks.' Andrew Card, his first chief of staff, argued that journalists 'don't represent the public any more than other people do. In our democracy, the people who represent the public stood for election.'[13] Both Bush and Card were right: the press does not represent the public; it represents what it defines as 'the public interest', a much argued-over concept, especially in the UK, where tabloid papers cite their much larger circulations as proof that they know what interests the public.

Obama, though, has a well-attested scorn for much of the press, and may be right in being scornful: he may be the first president who does not really need them. He may also be wrong – Mike McCurry, fair-minded, sees both sides of the issue, but on balance thinks the President is making a mistake.

I think Obama is playing on the disrepair that the profession is suffering, because he's almost openly disdainful of the press. He has these news conferences where he asks 'so and so' to ask a question as if he doesn't know who they are – but he does know. It is really clear that he chafes – every president has chafed. But before there was no choice: now you can self-publish.

In the last fortnight [December 2013] at the White House the photographers for the news organisations got very angry because the official photographer took all these wonderful pictures, as they were putting them up on the website and distributing them themselves. That's evidence of the decline in the press's stature: because if someone asked me when I was there what I would have made of that I would say I would never have dared try to get away with restricting access in that way. In fact I did a morning encounter in my office with them, we barked back and forth – and if they asked for some access I'd often say, I'll see what I can do. Part of my role was being a surrogate for them. That's not so now. I took the role seriously and it created good will because they felt they had someone on the inside batting for them.

The photographers in the White House reacted to the exclusion with anger: Santiago Lyon, the director of photography for the Associated Press, called the Obama White House 'undemocratic' and 'hypocritical' in the way it has 'systematically tried to bypass the media by releasing a sanitized visual record of [Obama's] activities through official photographs and videos, at the expense of independent journalistic access'.[14] However, the complaints had no effect. In February 2014, photographers were again shut out, this time from a meeting between Obama and the Dalai Lama: later, the press secretary Jay Carney said, 'You don't have to buy that newspaper or subscribe to that wire service to see that photograph' – a stark statement of the new era and the administration's determination to work within the new space it offers the President and his aides.

McCurry warns, however, that

the problem is that when you have no goodwill and capital in the bank, then when you have to make a withdrawal when something's wrong, then there's not a lot of love there to play on. There's not a symbiotic relationship which allows for understanding. So when Obama takes a tumble, like on the healthcare website, the press just gleefully kicks the shit out of him. It was just a website that wasn't working well: they turned that into a comment about the competency of the presidency.

The gulf is a serious one, defining presidential rapport with the news media, his and his aides' calculations on its importance and the level of power the press is still capable of wielding. In October 2013, the former editor of the *Washington Post*, Len Downie, did a report for the Committee to Protect Journalists, in which he argued that the administration was not only denying some access, but spreading a culture of fear around the bureaucracy to deter officials from talking to the press on any other than approved subjects, in an approved way. The report's preamble states:

> *U.S. President Barack Obama came into office pledging open government, but he has fallen short of his promise. Journalists and transparency advocates say the White House curbs routine disclosure of information and deploys its own media to evade scrutiny by the press. Aggressive prosecution of leakers of classified information and broad electronic surveillance programs deter government sources from speaking to journalists.*[15]

Downie quoted from a column by Margaret Sullivan, the *New York Times'* public editor, to the effect that 'it's turning out to be the administration of unprecedented secrecy and unprecedented attacks on a free press'.

The end of the announcement

When Ronald Reagan (in office 1981–9) gave his (rare) press conferences, the networks switched to them, postponing other programming. No one would do that now, unless they had been alerted that a critically important statement was to be made by the President. The White House, and politicians generally, are not directly responsible for that: the media, citing the boredom and cynicism of their readers, listeners, and viewers, cannot afford to prioritise such occasions.

However, the new technologies, as well as presidential desire to beat the press corps, are making announcements (again, apart from the near apocalyptic) seem increasingly old-fashioned. A new culture, that of the continuous conversation, even a continuous show, now begins to replace the regular or sporadic appearances of the chief executive, and other major political figures. Where continuous talk fills the airwaves of 24-hour news channels with little or no new news to impart, everything is reduced to mush – or, worse, to comment designed to provoke, not to inform.

Some of this emphasis on continuous chat is comically tedious. In a chat show on CNN in March 2014,[16] yet another conversation was taking place on what happened to the lost Malaysian Airlines flight 370. Retired general and CNN commentator James Marks, nicknamed 'Spider', said that he and his fellow panellists should cease their 'cacophony of conjecture' about the plane's fate, but 'get back to what we know and what we don't know'. The host, Bill Weir, laughingly intervened – 'You know how cable news works, Spider? We got time to fill here'.

One of the most persuasive advocates of the new conversation is not a political consultant, but the head of a large PR company which works only for corporate clients. Richard Edelman believes that 'the age of spin is over. A guy like Alastair Campbell – the master of spin – wouldn't work today, anyway not here [the US]. The time when "I'll talk when I damn well choose and I will control the message" – that's over.'

Drawing lines on a napkin, Edelman explains:

> I look at it now as two axes: one is the control axis, which is the vertical, and the other is the community axis, which is the horizontal. On the horizontal axis are the consumers, the NGOs, people who in one way or another are in the public arena. On the horizontal axis there are the CEOs, investors, government, regulators and so on. It's at the intersection of these two that truth is established. This conversation yields to the social: it is above all open.

Obama now goes on chat shows with Jay Leno and David Letterman, and many others; he lets himself be made fun of, and makes fun of others; he tweets (or someone tweets under his name). At the same time, he gives speeches marked by their seriousness and even complexity, though sometimes lacking in a clear conclusion, a defined course of action – more academic than executive. Disliking the press, Obama has almost casually, it seems, created enemies within it, including some of the most senior and respected among them, willing to say, as the *New York Times* reporter James Risen did in March 2014, that his administration is 'the greatest enemy of press freedom that we have encountered in at least a generation', with an ambition to 'narrow the field of national security reporting' and to 'create a path for accepted reporting'. Any journalist who exceeds those parameters 'will be punished'.[17]

At the same time, his aides have been hugely skilful in extending the social media reach of Obama, both as candidate and as President. Obama will be positioned as beginning a conversation with different groups – ethnic, gender-defined, professional, regional – and keeping these going interactively. It was a strategy partly inspired by the work the consultant Joe Trippi did for various Democratic hopefuls, including most famously Howard Dean, in his bid for the 2004 presidential nomination (though Dean fired him after the candidate lost Iowa and New Hampshire). Trippi, who believes that 'There is only one tool, one platform, one medium that allows the American people to take their government back, and that's the Internet', used it to raise hundreds of thousands of small donations to the Dean campaign – but also to 'converse' with his base, and to widen it by doing so.

The Republican consultant Kevin Madden concedes Obama's primacy in this area:

> *Everyone talks about the juggernaut that was the Obama campaign in 2011/12, and they're right, they deserve the praise ... campaigns used to be very top down, and it would be a very top down message – but for that campaign we knew it was going to be built from the bottom up, it was going to be won county by county and street by street, and that information was going to be shared from the bottom up. Now the thing is the conversation at the base. You're much more likely to vote for a candidate on the basis of the recommendation of people you know and respect in your community than you are on a 30-second ad. It's peer influence now.*

Says Edelman: 'What we now have is the creation of an inverted pyramid, that goes along with a classic pyramid of authority; now you have a pyramid of community, the mass of people at the top. The conversation is a diamond of influence. You can't any longer just talk down. You have to participate.' Obama is – ironically, to his increasingly exasperated observers in the press – trying to participate, in a way calculated to increase their exasperation.

Alastair Campbell, who handled communications for Prime Minister Tony Blair from 1997 to 2003, says:

> *You're no longer in a position to command and control. Before you could to an extent – events always came up – but there was a measure and*

sometimes a lot of control possible. The leader or the Prime Minister had the authority of his position and so that gave some control. You could control what he said and did.

You can't do it in the same way. Because someone with 20 followers on Twitter will put out something really significant – and it will be picked up by others with more followers – and Facebook – and then a paper – and so it goes. You can't control that.

But he adds:

I think that a tweet from a 25-year-old couldn't destroy a campaign unless it's destructible. So the example of Romney being upset by the tweet that he had told an audience that half the country were dependent on welfare played into an already existing view of him. There has to be an overall narrative into which something fits – even if it itself isn't true. But it 'feels true'.

The thing to be is proactive. Obama campaign – if they found a 25-year-old tweeting something they'd find out what he or she did, where he was, and try to enroll him into the campaign. When Clinton was under massive attack, they always managed to get their own voices out – they saw it as a strategic opportunity.

The end of humility

In a version of a Dickensian past, political consultants and corporate PR people both invoke a dark period where they were summoned from a dingy office, or even a cubicle, and told to put out a press release on an issue decided by executives or officials or politicians far above their grade. Not now. Says Joe Lockhart:

now when you want to make serious news you have to have a multi-platform strategy. That means you need people who can conceive a multi-platform strategy. When 30 years ago all you needed was someone who knew how to write a press release, and be nice to reporters, go out to lunch so you can call in a favour now and then.

But communications strategy was not central to corporate strategy, business strategy. Political strategy was a first mover there, that's where it all started. Even in 1980, 1984 when I started doing all this stuff, at the top comms people were nowhere to be seen. I don't care where you are now; any successful organisation has the comms people right there in the room, often driving it. The comms people have to have the ear of the top guy.

You see Ron Ziegler, Nixon's guy [press secretary from 1969–74] sent out to say whatever he was told to say. Without having any idea if it was true or not. Now in the White House, decisions are made with the comms guy sitting there and generally being a driver of the conversation.

Lockhart points to another development: not only have communications people become more powerful, they have ceased to be *only* communications people, while the policy people now no longer see a wall between them and their communications colleagues – because they are communications people too.

The people round Obama – David Axelrod and David Plouffe, and Karl Rove for Bush – they're all policy guys but they're also comms guys. More than 50% of politics now is your ability to communicate. Look at Obama's two senior advisers – both comms people. Axelrod was a journalist, then a comms person and moved into policy – and the same with Dan Pfeiffer who's got the job now [senior adviser for strategy and comms]. It's much more than the old school, going to lunch with reporters. It's become central to any successful strategy. It's a tribute to the success of the people who were the early movers – and in politics it probably started most distinctly with the Clinton campaign in '92 – which was all about comms.

As in corporate PR, political consultants now work more *as* journalists as well as *with* journalists. With a dedicated website for the candidate, as well as those run by supporters and allies, with hundreds of thousands of blog sites – not just those of supporters – desperate for new material, the present-day political consultant has channels of communication which can exceed the conventional news channels for all but very large events (or scandals) – with much less 'snarky' comment. Says Kevin Madden:

when it comes to where people are getting their information from online, I have this ability to create really unique persuadable, transactional content. I don't have to say, 'Golly gee, I really hope your paper can give me space on the op-ed page'. Instead I use our micro site to place out opinion/ commentary piece and then deliver it across a vast network

which I've built. It means I don't have to beg and plead any more. It
means I don't have to rely on the Rolodex any more.

This emphasis on social media is matched by – and is both stimulated by and stimulates – parallel developments in journalism. Says Siewert:

It felt like it started in the late nineties but it's taken off like a rocket in the last few years. It's upending the traditional hierarchy and career path of a journalist and of the news business. Not so long ago people of my age [50 in 2014] who wanted to rise in the news business worked diligently at some paper for 15 or 20 years as a reporter then as an editor then a higher-up editor. Nowadays the emphasis is much more on building a brand in digital and social media, and you are much less dependent on an institution. Nowadays people want to build a brand and get a profile on Twitter or on TV, so that's changed the system in the Wall Street Journal and the Post and the Times, and it's put a premium on creating a voice. Some places like the FT and the Economist and the New York Times try to beat that out of you, but broadly this is a different kind of journalism.

A different kind of journalism meets a different kind of communications – each sparking off each other, each blaming the other for the negative aspects of both the past and the present. What is now emerging is something like an electronic conversation – though with very large discrepancies in stature between those who take part in it. The lines between political communications and journalists are still there, but are becoming more blurred – as all meet on the internet, competing with commentary and with facts. Jay Rosen's mission to preserve a sense of what to trust and how to call to account can seem like Canute and the tide.

The end of lobbying? (Up to a point)

Washington has been so decisively the capital of lobbying, as the most powerful corporations in the world lobbied for influence on the most powerful government in the world, that it is disturbing to hear one marinated in the ways of the capital say, as Mike McCurry does, that it is largely over.

McCurry, with Joe O'Neill who had been chief of staff to Lloyd Bentsen, the Democratic senator, chairman of the Senate Finance

Committee, and for two years Treasury Secretary (1993–4), runs Public Strategies in Washington, which he said had had lobbying as one of its key offerings – since both the principals were extremely well connected. Now,

> very little of that classic lobbying practice exists any more. There was an assumption of guilt, and a predisposition against the powerful lobbyists. The Gucci-golf model isn't the way of getting things done any more.
>
> What's happened now is that power has shifted to those who, in a small 'd' democratic way, can access large networks of people and really influence public opinion in a dramatic way. You can go and make a good case to this or that corporation on this or that issue – but what's more powerful is to go and say: we've got 200,000 people who've signed our petition online and they really want you to do something on this issue; or we've mobilised the workforce and they're all writing letters asking for this change and demonstrating that this issue is the one they're really sensitive about.
>
> These new constituencies are mobilised by social networks and by powerful arguments – there has been a dramatic increase in the amount of money to pay people to go out to do research and to test messages and try to find what's the compelling argument. There's a huge increase in the money spent on public affairs using digital PR – on people who are really clever at developing things that go viral on the internet; an interesting argument or test case or some video that you can get out there and circulate it through social media, and people are responsive to that – so that lawmakers say: well there's a groundswell of support here at the ground-floor level. So the idea of grassroots mobilisation has become the golden coin for the people working at the Washington opinion business.
>
> There was stuff like this before of course. The famous case was a piece of banking legislation when all the banks in the country got their customers who were concerned about an increase in a transaction tax or something to send postcards to their members of congress and senators – one congressman said: well we didn't even read this mail, we just weighed it. [The issue[18] was a 1983 law which required banks to withhold 10% of interest income against tax: the Senate voted for a four-year postponement.] That was seen as powerful then, but now, the grassroots thing has really grown in significance and accelerated because you can leverage it with the high-speed tools of communication like Twitter.

This began to change our work in the White House when I was there – it is one of the most politically sensitive spots in this city – and anything that demonstrates sufficient public support is something you pay attention to, and it can be leveraged in a proactive way. Example: the '96 re-election campaign for Clinton – when the idea that we would have federal help to local school districts that wanted to have students wear school uniforms like they do in private schools here. When this was first announced, the White House people said: oh what a puny issue for the President.

But we knew through polling and research that there would be an enormous response to this – because people were concerned about kids stealing and getting mugged for a pair of sneakers or a sweater. It was the kind of thing you could generate a public response to – so getting adept at finding these hot-button issues that could generate a popular response became a significant part of the comms work of the White House and on down to local levels. That really began to change the nature of political comms: so much money had been spent on a TV 60-second spot – well, at a time when people are bleeping out the TV ads, the effectiveness of that kind of communications has begun to decline a little bit – and we're seeing a corresponding shift to the net, to elicit an emotional response. Now TV ads did that too – but it's become more difficult at a time when more people are skipping.

McCurry is probably overstating this. The big corporations have large interests for which they want either the support of or relief from government. Walmart, which does nearly all lobbying and PR in-house and which is one of the richest corporations in the world, keeps tight control of all communications, knowing that it will not escape being battered for the low pay to its employees, and the destruction of all competitors by its low-price, sell-everything strategy. Exxon Mobil is similarly huge – the richest and largest US oil company – and similarly closed to the press, similarly determined to control most of its own lobbying and PR. Both lobby continually.

Yet both corporations have also tried, with some success, to change and to take part in at least some conversations, dipping their giant toes in the new arena sketched out by Richard Edelman (whose firm advised Walmart). In 1996, Walmart employed the former Democratic communications consultant Leslie Dach, who had also lobbied for Audubon and the Environmental Defense Fund and was thus not an identikit Walmart executive, to be its executive vice president for corporate affairs and government relations. In an interview in July 2013 on leaving the company, Dach said, 'I think that the leadership made a fundamental decision that rather than just tell a better story, it would be a better business.'[19]

Dach, with a background in environmental work, pushed the company to develop a sustainable energy strategy and to create initiatives, like sourcing significant amounts of its products – $20bn was the target – from women-owned businesses. With Democratic credentials, Dach was hired when it became likely that a Democrat would win the next presidential election in 2008; and the initiatives he developed were those which Democratic legislators might be expected to favour. In all of these, the company engaged in active and public dialogues – some of which, on the respondents' side, were critical. It was a large shift from the behemoth slouching up to Pennsylvania Avenue with a request, or demand, for special or better treatment.

Exxon, an older company and one deeply invested in supporting the Republican Party, was more tentative.[20] It too, had tended to crouch down defensively when attacked for its environmental record; it was deeply distrustful of Obama, who attacked the oil companies vigorously when running for the presidency, and after – both on price and on environmental grounds. The company decided to change its strategy: it invited a Democratic aide and a consultant on corporate responsibility, Bennett Freeman, to address its senior executives. Freeman argued that the company had to develop alternative energy technologies: 'this is a carbon constrained future you're looking at'. The company did move down that road, replacing harder-line officials in sensitive posts with softer-edged ones, emphasising the ethnic diversity of their employees and their role in job creation during a recession; it invested in the Clinton Global Initiative, which channelled money to humanitarian causes in the world's poorest nations.

This seemed to help – its public approval ratings went up from 36 to 50%; but the commitment seemed less than that of Walmart. Crucially, the Freeman view on a carbon-constrained future seemed premature: Obama changed from an oil basher to an oil booster, boasting in his 2012 State of the Union address that oil imports had fallen by 10% in the previous year because of domestic energy supply – and saying that the problems of the production of alternative fuels would take at least a decade to solve. Exxon's power, and a changing environment, won out. It had only dipped a toe in the new water: the largest outcome seemed likely to be a lowered distrust of the Democrats, and something of a less rebarbative culture internally.

Yet both Walmart and Exxon remain vulnerable to the social-media-assembled crowds which McCurry describes: and while their products and (in Walmart's case) low prices remain important to the life of Americans, they must now be on their guard against a new form of opposition, which may be more powerful, and more influential on government, than in the past.

The end of the political oligarch? (Probably not)

This 'end trend' has a query after it because, though it is claimed (up to a limited point) by consultants, it does not seem over yet, nor even soon. The new techniques for getting the message across are also used by – or are used in tandem with – the raising of money for the voracious maws of American political campaigns. Joe Lockhart points to the use of

> analytical data-driven consumer marketing – it's what corporate America was doing before. Now the accepted wisdom is: data should drive everything – you need to both measure what you're doing and see what you're doing and the reaction to it with real hard numbers, with real analytical tools, allowing you to be much more precise and scientific.
>
> This is all from direct marketing, 20 years ago – when they went to see how 300 people reacted to an AB test [a test determining which of two almost identical variants a customer preferred, by incorporating one difference to determine which features were important]. They were selling steak knives that way. It allows the corporation or the campaign to drill down almost to the individual.
>
> The changes have been breathtaking – the tools we have are new, the concepts are not. What we're able to do now at a moment's notice is to drill down. It's direct mail – which was around when I got into politics. Direct mail was using voter files and zip code files, to be able to send a letter to someone which spoke just to them. This is in the 1980s – Richard Vickery and the Reagan revolution – they were able to do things that were revolutionary; they were on to something the Democrats weren't. Now it's quite changed – it's the comparison between the nuclear bombs used in 1945 and the abilities we have now. People are more likely to

respond when they hear from someone they know than someone they've never met.

Mike McCurry says:

people respond to what they see coming across their computer or iPad or increasingly hand-held device screen; and it's become a very important tool for fundraising because the cost of campaigns kept increasing. The Obama campaign showing you could run a broad-based campaign on small donors began to erode the power of the influence peddlers, who used to run fundraisers with $5,000 cheques rolling in – the power began to shift. You have to do both – small donors and big – but the extraordinary increase in the takings for the presidential campaign has come across because of the explosion of the small donors.

You feel like you can say no to wealthy donors more often – though I think that's in part a fiction because the folks that are in the high-end fundraising still do pretty well. And they get access to give their case on issues.

It has brought people to considering local issues more – though with no clear results on whether or not that changes the political dynamic yet: and the example of that is after the sporadic incidents of gun violence that seem to happen on a regular basis in the US – the gun control lobby has capitalised on that in a very regional way. They build support in these areas where the incident happened and get a lot of coverage locally – of course the big incidents have an effect nationally. And this applies to industries as well – if you want to get something done the trick is to attach something local to that which you want to get done nationally.

It is not to doubt the vigour of this movement to note that another, countervailing movement is also vigorous. In April 2014, the Supreme Court struck down limits on individual campaign contributions, allowing donors to support an unlimited number of candidates, arguing that the previous cap on contributions was an unconstitutional bar on free speech. Even before that, other Supreme Court judgments had progressively lifted other limits, allowing the development of Super PACs (Political Action Committees) and, using an income-tax loophole, the creation of non-profit 'social welfare' groups which can raise and spend money on campaigning without acknowledging the source. Because campaigns are so expensive – $1bn-plus each in the 2012 campaign for Obama and

Romney – fundraising is central to the presidential agenda. In the last two years of his first term, Obama held 194 fundraisers – more than his four predecessors combined had done in the same period: Ronald Reagan held three in that time.

Political consulting is in a febrile state, though not as febrile as that of journalism. Our examples have been drawn largely from the US, because it is there, as we have noted, that the most advanced techniques, driven by the largest spending, are being developed. The optimistic view, generally taken by consultants, is that the new technology will democratise campaigns, fundraising, and the office-holders running for elections themselves. Yet while the trends are unmistakable, their social and political outcomes are not.

The adversarial nature of political communications exposes a widening gap in PR provision. Political PR is essentially bipolar. If your candidate is up, your rival is down. If your message is resonating successfully with voters, your rival is failing. The entire machinery of communications is deployed aggressively against an election-campaign cycle. The messages last, at most, two campaign cycles before being consigned to political memoirs.

With a few exceptions, the attack-dog style of political PR is not replicated in the corporate world. In business and financial PR, success is measured less by grinding down competitor messages. In this advisory community, victory is more often defined by the rate of client acquisition compared with other agencies, rather than pushing an aggressive campaign on behalf of the client. Once a mandate is secured, the challenge is how to insert the client into a public conversation – one voice among many other competing voices – in a convincing way. In political PR, there is one ambition: to be the only voice heard.

In sum

- Political communication is traditionally a rough trade: inherited experience points to tactics which are ruthless, simplifying, portraying the opponent negatively and directed at the emotions rather than the reason. Much of this remains.
- The reporting of politics is changing, and taking new directions: the mainstream media continue much as before, though more personality-based and less well-resourced and trained; new niche startups

emphasise rigour and close investigation; others are zany, comic, and eccentric.

- The boundaries between various types of media are being lowered: politicians now must be constantly visible and audible.
- The political communicators have benefitted from the decline of the party, taking over much of the strategy of a campaign and preparing the public face of the candidate as well as the policies.
- Social media bring in larger real-time audiences who participate in campaigns, donate money, and put pressure on incumbents: political communications and journalism must remould themselves round the new activism.

4

How it's Done: the Internet as a Mechanism for a Changed Relationship between PR and Journalism

Pressure, power, and the new PR

Both PR and journalism are currently in a transition phase. Most key decision-makers at large media and PR firms are still pre-digital: they began their careers in an age of fax machines and first-generation PCs, and many find it hard to update. For them, the internet is still territory to explore, rather than to live in.

They are probing the medium from widely different perspectives. The media have approached digital distribution from a largely defensive stance, seeking to protect an economic model and experimenting with a variety of subscription or ad-funded revenue streams. For the media, especially print media, digital is hugely disruptive, forcing them to shift from paper-based or analogue-carried output into digital channels while continuing to safeguard what they can of the previous system which still enjoys demand, and meeting much greater competition while doing so.

For PR agents, digital is an exploratory opportunity: about new routes to market, new ways to manage and place content. It creates multiple platforms on which to push a message, often without the editorial checks and balances typical of the analogue-media age. Journalism, because of the much greater fixed costs in printing and broadcasting equipment and the power of the traditional media, has been slower to adapt to the digital revolution and it has also taken considerable time to adopt new methods of communication.

PR has taken a more savvy approach: an agile discipline, it has been quicker to recognise the value and challenges presented by the internet and the advent of social media. The new media world also presents opportunities for digital innovators and the market has become more competitive, with online marketing and media agencies offering new services that impact the remit of PR: these include online reputation management, search engine optimisation and content creation (including web design). New roles have also been created – such as head of digital, social media manager, and others – working alongside traditional PR personnel.

Journalism is now competing in a much broader market than before, where new publications such as the Huffington Post, and the many new specialist news and comment sites, can gain momentum and achieve influence that can rival the traditional and more established outlets. Social media are largely responsible for enabling greater access to readers, increased engagement levels, and wider reach. Perhaps most significantly, they also facilitate a two-way conversation between media and readers or brands and consumers.

There is an explosion of content. Newspapers, especially national papers, are under growing pressure to present information on multimedia platforms: in doing so, they increasingly provide video coverage, merging print and broadcast journalism. As they are presented with a greater number of options in output, consumers are becoming more demanding about the formats they require, which means multimedia journalism is growing in popularity. A combination of fast-moving lifestyles and developments in technology, such as the smartphone and its rapidly evolving apps, enables users to consume up-to-date information at the click of a finger: the market pressure privileges content which is concise and quick to digest.

With so much choice in the type of news and information provided, the reader has more power, while publishers are increasingly able to adapt content to suit user requirements through the use of analytical programmes available to digital media platforms producing detailed analyses of consumption habits (see below). This feeds through into content production, and gives much more accurate information to advertisers and public relations teams, providing technological insight into the influential publications. This assists with supporting the focus of the output by understanding the reach and value of content, maximising its commercial value.

Data brings journalists much closer to the market – a relationship which, in the past, they had been able to avoid, even to scorn. No longer. To enter the Telegraph Group newsroom is to be confronted with a large interactive board which relays instant web analytics to journalists, including the most popular story of the moment. This drives competition among staff journalists – and provides readership insight and highlights commercial opportunities.

There is pressure for the traditional mainstream titles to maintain leadership in the market, uphold influence, and stand out in a space that has become crowded and overloaded with information. However, rather than digital opposing traditional, the two are intrinsically dependent upon each other. The traditional press relies on the resources of digital to extend its reach and to make the transition, which all now believe inevitable, from print to the internet; while the success of digital remains reliant upon the influence and long-standing reputation of traditional media.

Paul Blanchard, Managing Director of Right Angles PR and Vice President of the Media Society, says:

> We are seeing situations where the traditional press includes comments from Twitter in news articles as first-hand sources. This gives credit to the Twitter user, or in some cases the blogger, and helps them to become an authoritative source. There is a reciprocal relationship between the social commentator and the national newspapers. The former welcomes the credibility to help them stand out in a crowded space and the latter is dependent on this type of news media or commentary to give additional and instant insight into certain news stories or events.

Social media have empowered journalism and reporting. Twitter lends itself well to news reporting by functioning as an early warning system – usually earlier than the news wires – and also by providing quotes. The character limit for tweets of 140 is further reduced with the addition of an image or link, which means that concise updates are required: the brevity of the messages means they can be retweeted and spread around the world within moments.

Twitter gives journalists, brands, and the public a voice, even if a brief one. Meanwhile, filtering messages through sorting mechanisms such as hashtags allows trending topics to be identified. For example, conversation about live football matches, a sudden natural disaster, or an election campaign can be grouped according to subject. Conversation can be streamed and influential figures are easily followed, providing the reader with direct access to a greater range of sources. Technology makes it easier to organise information, though this prompts the charge that it is, at the same time, dumbing it down.

Digital media have played an increasingly prominent role in breaking major news stories, while social media empower witnesses to key events to be reactive with comments that are published in the public domain.

Research by Osborne and Dredze concurs, 'Twitter has a reputation for being the first place to report on certain kinds of events, such as earthquakes or sports events. Out of the three main social media, it consistently carries news before either Facebook or Google Plus.'[1]

Twitter provides second-by-second accounts of news stories with real-time quotes, adding further verification to stories. Eyewitnesses to a large chalet fire in Val d'Isère in February 2014 recorded the incident on their iPhone and submitted the coverage to the BBC, which used it as their source whilst reporting the event in the main news bulletin. Thus the media have access to many more 'journalists', or at least contributors, in the form of a news-reporting public – the citizen journalists.

Publications that have traditionally led the way on breaking news are forced to adapt to suit the digital landscape; however, they are still maintaining a lead. According to the results of the Osborne and Dredze research, 'all public posts in social media streams carry similar events to each other. Yet Twitter dominates other social media in providing timely news. Still, Twitter lags newswire, which remains the best source for breaking news.'

Twitter is more reactive than some press agencies, but it does not have equal credibility: errors spread as speedily as fact. Errors can, of course, appear in press agencies' copy and in other legacy media, and the social media give these errors worldwide wings. In 2012, the wrong brother (Ryan Lanza) was named by press agencies and American media as the gunman responsible for the Sandy Hook massacre, in which a gunman opened fire in a school in Newtown, Connecticut killing six staff and 20 children. The misinformation spread rapidly via online media and through social media and became difficult to correct. The difference is that the legacy media have, or should have, a culture of checking and correction: none exists for Twitter.

The fact that paper-based media are out of date as soon as they are published in the traditional format means that they increasingly concentrate on setting the agenda and providing complex analysis and comment. Although the number of people who can publish stories through blogs and other online platforms has dramatically increased, the quality of journalists and commentary remains an important focus for the traditional newspapers and it remains, still, a unique selling point.

The first newspaper websites began as streamlined versions of the newspaper, a mere reflection of the print output. However, as the digital era progressed, online content took on a life of its own, which more closely resembled a 24-hour wire service than a traditional newspaper, in updating news and breaking stories. It also quickly realised it had to be different to its print equivalent. In an increasingly aggressive battle to win readership in a competitive market, traditional publications are pressured into producing a high volume of articles that are optimised for search engine results pages and appear highly in the rankings of certain search engines, chiefly Google (see below). This has caused them to leverage PR-generated content in some cases.

Technical strategies and information science aspects have become more important. Search engine optimisation and reputation management have been pushed to the fore. The 2014 Edelman Trust Barometer highlighted:

> When it comes to first sources of information, respondents rated online, newspapers and television relatively evenly for both general business information and breaking news about business. The tables turn for breaking news, where television leads newspapers by five points, while newspapers lead television slightly for general information. Online is most trusted for both types of information.

Furthermore, the Barometer revealed that online is now surpassing other media for trust in several aspects: 'Perhaps more revealing than level of trust in sources for first finding information is level of trust in sources for confirming or validating information about business. On this question, respondents rated online search significantly higher than television and newspapers.'

As online information becomes more powerful, it is important to acknowledge the new gatekeepers when seeking news content. One new gatekeeper is the search engine and the fight to own the top positions of the search engine results pages has become more important and relevant to both media and PR strategies.

Making a success of online journalism

Newspaper strategies at present split between offering all or most of their content free, and protecting it with a pay wall, allowing only subscribers to access the material. Of the very few which have no pay wall, and make a profit, the Mail Online stands out as the most popular English-language website in the world. It turned a profit for the first time in 2012:[2] but even huge audiences do not guarantee commercial revenues. In spite of its reach, the newspaper's web-based platform generates only a fraction of the advertising income that is delivered by the newspaper.

Rather than simply producing high-value content for readers in the new media world, newspapers need to consider the search engine algorithms. Search engine algorithms reward technical aspects, such as the optimisation of a website; they also reward websites that produce significant amount of fresh news or articles, in a format of over 300 words, with varied keywords that are not hidden behind a pay wall. A brief technical analysis of the Mail Online website indicates that search engine optimisation (SEO) is clearly an important element of their strategy.

Technical dynamics of the new media world

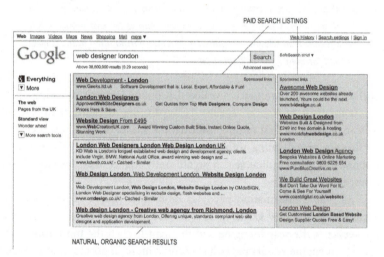

Diagram 4.1. An example of a Google search page (http://www. searchcatalyst.co.uk).

NATURAL, ORGANIC RESULTS: Organic search results are listings on search engine results pages that appear because of their relevance to the search terms, as opposed to their being advertisements. In contrast, non-organic search results may include pay per click advertising.

PAID SEARCH LISTINGS: The Pay Per Click (PPC) advertising model is used for the top section of the search engine results pages. This features above the organic search results. The PPC model is a method of directing internet browsers to certain websites and is a way for advertisers to pay a publisher when the ad is clicked. Many brands will bid on certain keywords and phrases that are commonly entered into the query box, in an attempt to feature at the top of the listing for their target market and attract a potential customer to click through to their website.

The science of search engine optimisation has existed for many years. Although it has evolved to incorporate a number of factors, the chief focus concerns the process of manipulating the visibility of a website or a web page in the organic search results that appear in a search engine. The organic results are those achieved without commissioning a specific listing. An SEO company will be paid to implement the manipulation and this involves taking advantage of Google's algorithm to improve the authority of a company's web pages.

Although SEO practitioners influence the results of search engines like Google and Bing, the activity is acknowledged as an important element of any digital strategy. It is a practice that is accepted by search engines; however, there are certain guidelines in place to encourage, though not always achieve, an ethical approach.

The amount of traffic a news or consumer website receives is a crucial factor for e-commerce as each hit has the potential to convert to a purchase. Traffic is also important for determining the advertising reach of publications. A simple example of the deployment of SEO: during a heat wave, there is likely to be an increase in the amount of people looking to buy a cool box. Major supermarkets may begin to bid on the search term 'where to buy a cool box' using pay per click (PPC) to secure the top space of Google's paid-for listings. This will encourage users to click on to the supermarket to buy their item.

The supermarket may also begin a wider marketing campaign that will help their website to rank more highly in the organic search results. Activity that suits the search engine guidelines includes the generation of high-quality content and also engaging social media activity. Therefore, the supermarket will aim to be part of the conversation and a strong provider of editorial content. While coverage in media outlets is helpful, the chief focus is a much broader proliferation of the brand message that reaches beyond traditional media. This involves creating effective social media campaigns by leveraging Twitter, Facebook, and Instagram, in order to extend the reach of the product message. It also includes encouraging relevant bloggers to write high-quality content. Google's guidelines are intended to assist with the ethical generation of information and to deter spam. With this in mind, companies creating spam content may be penalised by losing their high-ranking positions. An intelligent content outreach strategy is required, focusing on quality content.

Google is presently the unchallenged king of search engines, though it has a propensity to change its policies and algorithms regularly to capitalise on commercial opportunities. One SEO expert, who preferred not to be named, explained the history of changes that specifically relate to SEO and PPC:

> About a decade ago it was possible for brands to bid on competitive terms. For example, major supermarkets would be able to outbid each other in regard to their own names. Google was writing its own cheques, with huge corporates stuck in fierce bidding wars. Hypothetically, you could have a situation whereby Tesco pays to rank for the search term Morrisons and vice versa. However, Google decided to ban this from happening – but not for long! Although there was a period of time whereby you could not bid on competitive terms, this is now possible again to some degree, netting Google a large sum of money, again.

Bidding wars meant that major businesses were bidding against each other for their own brand to seize the first spot of the PPC rankings in Google, with brands needing to spend money on certain search terms, including their own name. One marketing manager at a global fashion brand explains:

> If we want to ensure our brand features at the top of the page on Google, we have to bid on our own brand name as a search term. Whoever is willing to pay the most money per potential click [this fluctuates greatly for many different reasons but can be anything from 10p to 70p for 'brand'] will come out on top. There are now some factors such as the relevance of the site that help to prevent bidding wars with rival brands from escalating as the content of the site also helps you reach top spot. However, this is not always effective at preventing competitors from outranking you.

While tweaks to the algorithm provide some respite for brands, Google is still cashing in on the competitive retail market. Some companies feel forced into a situation whereby they have to pay money for their own name to appear at the top of the paid search. The source continues:

> *If we do not bid on our own brand name, we leave ourselves exposed to a rival brand ranking ahead of ours when users are searching for us. We become very vulnerable. Google is laughing; although we see return on owning the first position, our outgoing spend can be as much as £4,000 per week to occupy this space.*

Other brands will be paying similar fees, if not substantially more, and Google has control over the marketplace, with no other search engine currently rivalling its monopoly.

While there is a high spend allocated by many brands to online marketing and PR, there is no doubt that it brings a strong return. The intricate level of analytical data is responsible for positioning this new form of advertising ahead of traditional PR strategies. Brands can track the amount of conversions they receive from bidding on certain key words and banner advertising. 'Above the line' marketing (such as an advert on a bus) is difficult to value, whereas the analytical data that is available from online methods mean that marketing strategies can be tailored and the success of the outgoing spend is traceable.

Google is providing an attractive alternative to traditional PR, which is at times preferable. The source comments:

> *I would much rather have our fashion brand permanently appearing at the top of Google for a search term such as 'black dress' than have a one-off double-page spread in the Sunday Times. We have an almost 30% annual growth in the online side of the business and bidding on key search terms – such as 'black dress' – is an important part of that growth.*

Publications with progressive websites, such as the Mail Online, have been clever in capitalising on online sales, particularly in fashion. Recent developments to their website allow users to read an article about Kate Moss and then view a selection of the items that she is wearing. If the reader follows through and purchases from the recommended brands, an affiliate marketing fee (a percentage of the product sale) can be received.

Search engines want to encourage PPC as a good way of generating revenue. Questions are sometimes raised as a result of the technical updates made to the algorithms, which some argue appear to favour those brands that are paying search engines for PPC. The SEO expert commented on the roll-out of one such update: 'There have been observations within the SEO community that the update favoured big brands, which means that smaller brands are pushed into paying for PPC to secure visibility.' So it seems that the organic listings may not be so organic.

However, Google has implemented certain guidelines to encourage the declaration of sponsored content and this is designed to help prevent paid content from influencing the rankings in the organic search results section. The algorithms used by search engines are becoming more sophisticated; however, this is a work in progress and there are still loopholes.

SEO experts will normally wish to leverage social media, since a website gains additional authority through including a large amount of social sharing, indicating as it does to a search engine that the material is popular, relevant, and positively consumed. This activity can become relevant to news websites: while social shares are expected for news articles, an SEO-aware publication may consider massaging the popularity of certain stories as part of their marketing strategy to ensure their coverage ranks at the top of the page. In such an instance, computer-generated social media accounts will be instructed to distribute the content to make it appear more popular and to help it gain higher authority.

Search engines are trying to incorporate social signals into their algorithms. Although these signals impact the results on a relatively small scale, in time it will become more important to run a sophisticated social media project in line with an SEO project to maximise results.

Where SEO is used on media websites that are looking to increase their readership, articles are often written in web-optimised versions and contain trending keywords that drive current traffic to the website through search. A high volume of articles are published throughout the day to attract return visitors. This could be seen during coverage of the 2014 royal tour of Australia and New Zealand by the Duke and Duchess of Cambridge, when multiple articles were created about the same topic, which would have suited trending keywords on search engines. Although Mail Online clearly uses SEO in its internet approach, it is also widely noted that it has recorded such significant traffic due to a focus on celebrity stories, high picture content, and a growing appeal to an American audience. These factors have become as important as the news agenda.

Furthermore, Mail Online appears to utilise the increase in content that is delivered directly to news desks by PR agencies (see below): in particular, consumer-focused content. Press releases – albeit with modifications – can be used as a basis for some of the articles, obviating updates from journalists, and placing the content more firmly in the PR camp.

Making the model pay

Mail Online can command relatively high advertising fees from brands seeking a presence on its website, attracted by the high number of daily visits. Yet making the free-content model pay is not easy: a problem felt by the *Guardian*, which has also championed free content accessible to all.

In contrast to the Mail Online, the *Guardian* is less inclined to overtly leverage the content provided directly by PR; however, there are indications of a change. One well-positioned PR source in a leading firm has cited the direct placement of a story in the *Guardian* and also admitted that this would not have been possible several years ago.

While some publications opt for paid content, the *Guardian* prioritises access as this remains important for readers. Simon McCall is Director of Boxwood's Technology, Media and Telecoms sector and played a role in advising how the *Guardian* should amend its business model. He highlights one of the new methods that can assist with commercialising the free-access model which the *Guardian* has retained: 'Advertising, sponsorship, branded applications and leveraging the brand is now more important.'

This means there is growing convergence between the commercial needs of online media and the appetite of businesses – and their PR counsel – to place sponsored content online. Working with PR is vital for the success of online journalism and has become more powerful in the digital age. This has consequences for the differentiation between editorial and advertorial.

While emerging publications can provide valuable commentary, the influence of traditional publications and the value of their journalists are crucial for maintaining authority. However, publications like the *Guardian* cannot rely on reputation alone for brand protection and need to consider data. Google Analytics and Omniture (now owned by Adobe) are examples of tools that allow detailed data to be collected from most web browsers. While it is possible to adjust privacy settings and browse websites anonymously, many users are oblivious to such controls, or simply do not care about their data being collected. This means that online publications can become more informed about their audience.

Demographic data that can be retrieved from a single visit to a website include the age, gender, interests, language, and location of the visitor. Such data can be collected over a sustained period and can be viewed in real time; they can prove helpful when monitoring popular interest in certain breaking news stories, as in the *Telegraph* offices. It is also possible to organise filters according to keywords, IP addresses, and to map user behaviour by understanding the pattern of a visitor. This empowers online publishing platforms with the ability to manipulate certain attributes of their website to maximise readership or sale conversion. For example, the style of the landing page, positioning of certain links or articles, and focus of specific content can all attribute to a growth in readership or sales.

While the mass-market approach that involves attracting high readership statistics, free content, and a plethora of expansion opportunities is championed by some, the pay wall model is growing and provides a space for targeted publications to flourish. It has also become important for PR companies to place content in both volume media reaching mass audiences and niche high-value outlets, which claim to reach more select opinion-formers.

Gosia Brzezinska works as an account manager across a number of political accounts at Portland Communications and describes this type of coverage as 'posh coverage'. She says that 'it's seen as posh coverage because it is not available to everyone; publications such as *Foreign Affairs* are perceived to have an elite audience'.

The pay wall approach mirrors the traditional forms of media more closely and requires paying a subscription fee to access articles in preferred publications, which is similar to purchasing a hard copy of the newspaper. It creates a sense of elitism in the digital media world.

Even online subscriptions do not guarantee revenues to match the traditional mix of cover price and print advertising. There remains a question over whether the growth in online subscribers and related advertising will be fast enough to compensate for the rate of decline in circulation and print-ad sales. Jeff Zucker, President of CNN, has described the dilemma as 'trading analogue dollars for digital dimes'.

There is still confusion in the digital media industry as to which approach works best. Regardless of which model is championed, online journalism does expect a different output: it is an arts profession (journalism) merging with a scientific profession (computer science). PR also plays a crucial role in this relationship and the all-encompassing digital strategy is now becoming an essential offering.

A blur between advertorial and editorial

The mass-market approach has opened a whole new world of opportunity from a commercial perspective and this challenges the relationship between journalism and PR, as the lines between editorial and advertorial become blurred. As McCall highlights:

> In a world that is swamped by advertising how can we know what is real? That is where the intelligence of the major brands comes into play and where journalists play an important role. As more content becomes PR-driven and hidden advertising is occurring, journalists have a role to play in telling the truth and revealing the raw stories to readers. Quality journalism and brand values are therefore very important. This is crucial to the survival of journalism.

However, the digital era is changing the way editorial and advertorial is structured. As we have seen, the *New York Times* sparked controversy early in 2014 by unveiling a new advertising model that allows sponsored posts to sit alongside editorial. Ideally the distinction between paid and unpaid content should be clear: that, though, is not always the case; sponsored features is one way that PR is approaching the digital media world to secure coverage.

Disguising paid content is not uncommon. One highly regarded fashion PR explained that certain publications will accept previews of new collections from a fashion house or department store on the basis that the brands pay a placement fee. The reader is not always made aware of the advertorial relationship.

A documentary by Channel 4's investigative current affairs programme, *Dispatches,* highlighted the growing trend of PR agencies gifting celebrities with products in exchange for an endorsement via social media.[3] PR executives were recorded specifically asking celebrities to tweet in exchange for certain products.

Several articles[4] have addressed the issue of suspicious-looking tweets that have been released by celebrity icons in America, such as Kim

Kardashian and Justin Bieber. Kardashian has over 20 million followers and Bieber has over 50 million followers. Particular examples include the former tweeting about a lip balm from a cosmetics company during her pregnancy and the latter recommending a flower company on Mother's Day to his followers – neither declared the tweets as advertisements. These celebrities have used social media to escalate their profile and have a huge following on Twitter, with a high engagement level. Consumer PRs acknowledge the influence of such reach and attempt to negotiate access to the audience. The Federal Trade Commission maintains that the responsibility lies with the brand to ensure their influencers use the appropriate language when endorsing products.

In the UK, Wayne Rooney and Nike became the subject of such a controversy in 2012. The footballer released tweets from his account with a Nike marketing hashtag and a link to the brand's website. Complaints were received by the Advertising Standards Authority; the Authority commented:

> We considered there was nothing obvious in the tweets to indicate they were Nike marketing communications. In the absence of such an indication, for example #ad, we considered the tweets were not obviously identifiable as Nike marketing communications and therefore concluded they breached the code.[5]

The inclusion of hashtags such as #ad or #sponsored to indicate paid content is difficult to police and the responsibility lies with the brand, rather than the influencer. Brands do not always communicate the requirement for a hashtag to those endorsing products.

While there is no open agreement and the suggestion of guaranteeing press coverage is rarely directly posed to a journalist, gifting products is considered a key way of increasing the chance of coverage. The blogging sector in particular involves many individuals writing as a hobby and receiving reward for their work through gifting: this acts as an incentive to write about a brand. Many bloggers claim that reviewing consumer products is essential for writing a balanced and informative feature and in no way secures preferential coverage or coverage at all. The author of the popular lifestyle blog The Londoner is a full-time blogger and makes money from her blog. Although she welcomes items being sent, she also makes clear that 'I'm afraid I obviously can't promise to write about it on the blog.'

A similar situation occurs in retail, where gifting celebrities is a common yet canny PR strategy. Major fashion brands will gift celebrities in order to achieve the widespread coverage of an 'influencer'. If a celebrity wears an item of clothing, they are likely to put a picture on their social media accounts and also get 'papped' for the traditional media. As one well-placed source (who chose to remain anonymous) explains, 'This doesn't get classed as bribery as there is no suggestion made to the celebrity that they should wear the clothing. However, if you gift someone a number of items, there is high chance they will end up wearing the product, get photographed and provide us with great coverage.'

Paul Blanchard explained that it is not unusual for journalists to benefit financially from a PR arrangement. In such an instance, a PR representative will suggest that a company commissions a journalist or an editor to write a feature. The journalist will then submit the same feature for publication and is paid by both parties. This is most common with specialist publications that relate to certain industries. The journalist is never asked to submit the piece and never asked to provide positive coverage – in many cases it may not result in an entirely positive piece – and, therefore, does not consider it a breach of ethics. Journalists are becoming wiser about a PR-led market in which they can earn additional fees.

The impact of the internet on public relations

PR is faced with a challenging landscape for clients – but also many more commercial opportunities. As a junior PR professional, James Thomlinson recognised the need for a dedicated digital team at Bell Pottinger. After eight years of working in traditional PR within the company, he was asked to evaluate their digital strategy. This was ultimately driven by a need from clients for a multifaceted approach to communications, covering a broad stream of content and not just traditional print media. Thomlinson pitched the formation of Bell Pottinger Wired to the Board, and the digital arm of the company was duly formed. He is now Managing Director of Bell Pottinger Wired and, although there is much collaboration across the group, it remains a segregated unit.

Thomlinson says that 'More of our clients understand the pressure of the internet better. It is no longer just about a PR brief but a communications brief, where all areas are covered. This can include events, lobbying and digital content such as videos, website creation and apps. The market has begun to consolidate.'

Bell Pottinger Wired assists with the digital needs of clients; however, during recent years, the approach has become more integrated across a vast array of campaigns. From web-content creation to SEO, those instructing public relations companies have begun to request much broader services than those which are centred on press exposure and managing a media profile, especially in crisis management and risk mitigation.

One of the most notable areas of growth is reputation management. Fresh eyes have been cast over reputation in the last year, driven partly by the risks associated with a fast-moving digital media world. There are dedicated technical companies that support this area of internet communication (see below) and reputation is moving towards the top of the agenda.

The nature of online communication is the main reason that reputation has resurfaced as a prominent issue. News is breaking more quickly than ever before and this can impact the reputation of a company in many ways. A negative impression can escalate through social media via the power of rapid distribution. Many public companies and newsworthy individuals are now placed in a vulnerable position with regards to crisis management and reaction time.

A discussion with Mark Bolland, former private secretary to the Prince of Wales, highlights the importance of time management. He points out that while there used to be a period of time – often days – where people could wait before responding to a crisis situation, this has now been dramatically reduced and there is less opportunity for those in senior communications positions to assume there is time to plan an elaborate response. The right reaction needs to happen and it needs to happen quickly. Most interestingly of all, with the advent of a 24/7 media, there *needs* to be a reaction; avoidance is no longer considered acceptable.

Twitter, like all social media, can rebound on its users. In 2013, JP Morgan attempted to use Twitter to encourage the community to ask direct questions of the company. The strategy involved using the hashtag #AskJPM, which was unique to the exercise and highlighted the conversation to the public. The #AskJPM hashtag spread rapidly and attracted wider press attention as thousands of Twitter users sent tweets with negative responses and used the hashtag to make the conversation as visible as possible. These included insults, reference to corporate responsibility and the banking crisis, as well as JP Morgan's legal issues. Spokesman Brian Marchiony later commented, 'Bad idea! Back to the drawing board.'

In the service industry Twitter requires monitoring and management; however, in the corporate environment, the company can simply refuse to use it, or discourage a specific topic of conversation. Allan Biggar, former Chairman of Burson-Marsteller and now a partner at Jericho Chambers, believes, however, that it is better to take part than not:

> Technology has allowed people to ask and talk directly to a company or CEO and they should respond. This is why there needs to be an authentic approach to PR and communications. The world is highly transparent and the barrier has been removed. You need to teach and train people how to communicate. It is important to help them spread the message and get involved.

At Portland, Brzezinska concludes that technology has caused a blur between corporate and personal reputation:

> Technology enables access at all levels and this means there is a need to care for the corporate reputation and personal reputation. Companies are becoming much more accessible by opening their communication channels and it is not just the PR team that is controlling the message. There is a much wider level of communication in relation to outward interaction.

Individuals and organisations are regularly bombarded with negative commentary; they can, however, avoid the worst by learning how best to use social media. Timing is crucial; if you comment using a popular generic hashtag, the backlash is likely to be less visible than when using a unique hashtag. For example, if David Cameron comments on an issue relating to the UK budget and uses the general #budget hashtag, his comments are likely to become hidden among a sea of other activity surrounding this topic. However, if Cameron was to create his own hashtag, for example #CameronsBudgetViews, any negativity would be much more prominent. If a negative theme develops (which is common with 'Twitter Trolling'), it can snowball and attract significant attention.

Hashtags can also be hijacked. One such incident occurred on the day preceding the European Elections in May. UKIP created the hashtag #WhyImVotingUkip for party members to express their reasons for voting and also encourage the conversation to trend. The conversation became a trending topic after the hashtag was hijacked and Twitter users began to use it to poke fun at the party. Examples included:

> #WhyImVotingUkip: because, like the leader @Nigel_Farage, I get a bit racist when I'm tired too.
> #WhyImVotingUkip Because the weather's really starting to pick up, and I don't want it ruined by gays.

The latter was retweeted nearly 3,000 times.

British Gas experienced a negative issue when they used the #AskBG hashtag shortly after an increase in energy prices was announced. The idea was to engage with customers and allow them to ask questions about any concerns they had. A Twitter storm followed and thousands abused the company with negative tweets and caused the issue to feature as a trending topic in the news media.

Engaging in a live Twitter discussion using such an openly accessible platform requires careful consideration. Mistakes are sorely punished and there is a substantial risk of a PR disaster occurring.

Yet Biggar is right: abstaining from social media activity can prove detrimental in a crisis situation. BP was heavily criticised for its lack of engagement via Facebook, YouTube, Twitter, and blogging channels. Instead, the company spent large amounts of money on an SEO strategy and standard marketing practice.

By contrast, fashion brand DKNY excelled when handling a difficult situation in 2013. A popular blog accused DKNY of using copyrighted photos without prior permission. 'DKNY PR Girl' ran the account (which now has a following of over 400,000) and gained a reputation for excelling in Twitter responses with her natural and reactive manner. She showed her strengths when addressing the situation directly as anger began to flare up and gather momentum. Admitting DKNY were at fault, apologising, and then announcing a substantial donation to the Brooklyn YMCA, they reversed the tone of the crisis within moments. What was originally considered threatening to the brand's reputation actually triggered widespread recognition: the example is regularly used as a positive case study.

Roland Rudd, founder of Finsbury, says that time pressure can impact fluidity. It certainly forces greater transparency and a refined communication strategy, which encompasses risk prevention and risk mitigation. This need is fundamentally driven by the heightened dangers of transparent communication and the exposure that technology brings. The digital landscape plays into the hands of the PR industry.

Biggar at Jericho Chambers says that a multi-resourced and trusted team is part of the new PR model that is emerging:

> Twenty years ago the media world was very different and it used to be about the PR and journalist only. Now there is an opportunity to get the CEO and Board of Directors talking directly. We consider this as a huge opportunity to engage directly with the stakeholders rather than producing an over-packaged product. Shareholders want to hear directly from the company and offering an integrated PR approach is vital.

The emergence of brand journalism and recreational journalism

The focus and expectations of both PR and journalism are changing in the digital era. PR companies are required to offer broader services and journalists are expected to provide a greater variety of content. It is also now common for corporations to provide their own digital channels and this often involves appointing internal communications teams. The internal communications team traditionally includes PR and marketing personnel; however, journalists are now also incorporated into the structure: 'brand journalism' is becoming more widespread.

This trend of communication is most common with major consumer brands. Brand journalism allows the company to tell a story and to distribute the story directly to consumers via multimedia channels. While most consumers recognise the story is not always objective, both PR professionals and journalists who are looking to capitalise on the financial gain of working for a large corporate are maximising the value of such an opportunity. As trust in the media declines, this direct method of communication provides an acceptable alternative approach for many companies.

Red Bull is one example of a brand that merges PR, online communications, and journalism as part of a powerful, independent strategy. Their collaboration with extreme sports enables a unique level of passive engagement with readers. The Red Bull website offers informative articles about Formula One; they maximise the commercial collaboration with certain sports by creating news portals that offer features and commentary about racing. This further engages readers and the additional coverage adds more value for the sports fan; however, this coverage is supported and hosted by a brand, rather than a media publication.

The clothing company Burberry became the most talked-about brand on Twitter during London Fashion Week in 2013 as it pioneered a new approach to coverage. Those following the brand on Twitter were offered exclusive content, such as behind-the-scenes photos of each look, moments before it was presented to the audience on the catwalk – even before the press. For the Womenswear S/S14, Burberry used a Twitter Card to livestream the show, backed by Promoted Tweets and Promoted Accounts, to increase its follower base.

Aside from innovative social-media messaging that is driven directly by fashion brands, these companies also leverage social media use via influencers. For example, British model Cara Delevingne's rapid rise in the fashion industry has been largely attributed to her social media activity and following. *British Vogue* tagged her as 'the model who was *liked* into superstardom' on their January 2014 cover, which was a nod towards her Instagram following where fans can *like* her images (her followers currently stand at an impressive 5,012,436). She also has over 1.61 million followers on Twitter and when she collaborates with big brands, such as Chanel, Mulberry, or Burberry, the model tweets behind-the-scenes footage from the photo-shoots or catwalks to all of her fans and also distributes this via Instagram.

More and more brands understand that they can tell their stories as their own stories, whether this is directly via corporate channels or through a selected spokesperson. James Thomlinson of Bell Pottinger Wired argues that the media can become redundant in specialised areas with a clever PR strategy that utilises journalism traits: 'With a focused audience you don't necessarily need media.'

PR and journalism are both poised between the old world and the new – with some claiming that digital has or will soon take over, others pointing to the still important role mainstream media play. Thomlinson continues: 'You will always need the media because people want news. Third-party news and opinion is important. If a journalist writes about a story then this acts as an endorsement.' Paul Blanchard agrees:

> *There is a symbiotic relationship between the traditional media and social media and both are dependent upon each other. Journalists are now sourcing stories from the likes of Twitter and also using it as a source for quotes. Equally, there is so much information on social media, including*

Twitter. For a user to stand out from the crowd, the reply or the endorsement of traditional media is required. The traditional media can give significant power to a social media campaign, but the traditional media also find it a beneficial source.

Blanchard gives an example of mutual dependence from his own campaign – to ban foie gras, a pâté produced by force-feeding geese until their livers burst. He began spreading the word via social media and gained sufficient traction for a small campaign. However, once the traditional media picked up on the story, the campaign grew and delivered more users towards Twitter, who then spread the word even further through retweeting the handle and site links. Social media can gain significant traction alone, but once it is recorded in the traditional media, Blanchard explains, the scope and power will dramatically increase. The influence of newspapers and publications still offers value and credibility, thus remaining a crucial element of PR strategies.

Although the concept of brand journalism is becoming an increasingly popular and successful way of reaching the target audience in consumer PR, companies continue to seek neutral endorsement. Thomlinson cited a meeting with Huffington Post as one example where they discussed a partnership with a travel company. The travel company wanted to access a new market and was in need of quality content – which the Huffington Post could provide. Orchestrating collaboration between the two meant there would be a more powerful combined communications strategy to achieve greater leverage.

Brands value strong editorial, so journalists are attracted to the new medium – the more so as traditional media work becomes scarcer and less well paid. Social media assist with the facilitation of brand journalism and enable readers to follow a journalist, rather than a publication. This gives greater power to the journalist and personal branding is now playing an important role. Just as Cara Delevingne can empower a fashion brand, a journalist can empower a publication.

An example: author and columnist Caitlin Moran has over 491,000 followers on Twitter (April 2014), which exceeds both *The Times* (over 182,000) and the *Sunday Times* (over 193,000) combined. Those with a substantial following on Twitter and high engagement levels with their audience are now worth more to publications. Journalists are naturally strong communicators and therefore have the ability to leverage Twitter and use it to create conversation, spread their message, and ignite debate.

Journalists have an innate ability to react to the environment in order to best communicate with an audience. They also have access to verified news sources and an established network.

The issue of who owns the brand, however, is a live one for the BBC. Journalists are expected to tweet in a professional capacity for the Corporation, but with an individual profile as it enables a more streamlined feed (for example, certain correspondents can comment on relevant issues). One former BBC correspondent – who chose to be unnamed – explained that the BBC requested that all journalists have a Twitter account that is associated with the BBC: once they leave the Corporation, they are no longer allowed to use the account and, if they wish to continue tweeting, must launch a new one. While the digital society has enabled individual journalists to gain more traction and independent sway, they are considered credible in the first instance due to the endorsement of the media outlet, such as the BBC.

The media still maintain an important role in validating and approving information from other sources and reinforce influence by giving such sources credibility. How long this remains the case is questionable. The internet presents the opportunity for a journalist to break away from the umbrella of a publication and launch their own commercial venture and in turn presents a risk to the long-term survival of media publications.

Twitter users can often be more interested in following the journalist than the actual publication. Twitter rewards dynamic tweets and this can be easier to achieve when tweeting as a person rather than a company – this is relevant for both journalists and PR advisers. Blanchard elaborates, 'No one wants to follow the corporate machine and personality is important on Twitter – the person needs to be interesting.' Such parameters suit media individuals and certain sectors; however, engaging on Twitter can prove more challenging for those in the financial industry and many shy away from tweeting because of the potential risks involved.

Tweeting risks proliferate. Blanchard referred to a Twitter account that has been created to automatically detect deleted tweets by MPs: the account will immediately retweet the content to ensure it receives exposure. This means mistakes are highlighted and it becomes impossible to completely retract a statement. The riskiness of the medium means that Twitter accounts of CEOs, politicians, and others in public life are often controlled by a PR representative with expertise in this area who masquerades as the individual.

Individual influence is highly valued in consumer PR. Max Dundas formerly worked with Freud Communications before setting up his own boutique consultancy, specialising in brand, media, and celebrity PR. Over the years, he noticed that certain celebrities and public figures now have a greater pull than some of the leading traditional media outlets. Dundas Communications now places value on social media statistics for both a high-profile individual and also a publication. If a celebrity has a significant following (hundreds of thousands), they may have a greater influence in some capacities than some of the traditional leaders in the tabloid market, such as the *Sun* or *Mirror*. This directly impacts the type of coverage and impact of a PR strategy. For example, in some cases, a sponsorship deal or collaboration with an individual may reach an audience that is preferred to coverage in a newspaper.

Twitter is presently the hottest of social media: though other online networks have proven to be influential – such as Facebook and Instagram – Twitter remains more highly valued by most PRs, especially financial PRs. This is largely due to its format, which focuses on outgoing statements, with a lower level of social networking than Facebook. Rudd comments, 'Twitter is the biggest thing to come from social media: everything is always on Twitter first.'

Twitter has so far been able to escape the pitfall of overkill on advertising: Facebook, by contrast, has experienced problems with trying to charge businesses for exposure by changing its algorithm. Whereas a business page would historically have a high reach potential for fans, with updates appearing in newsfeeds of those who like the page, Facebook is now encouraging businesses to pay for their content to feature in the newsfeeds of fans. This has prompted grumbling: higher value is seen in Twitter, which does not yet penalise unsponsored content.

The advent of social media has enabled 'recreational journalism' by allowing anyone to publish material, gain a following, and become influential in a certain area. As Biggar comments, 'The media world has changed. Newspapers were a rich man's game but now anyone can stick on a laptop and create a news channel.' This has led to a new landscape of blogs and websites that are not run by professional journalists but still have influence in some markets. Certain feature blogs play a significant role in the approach to PR and communications for some clients.

The digital space is increasing the amount of content that is available and it is also enabling highly specialised content to emerge. Such new arenas need careful consideration. Thomlinson says, 'The media are typically very generalist whereas bloggers are very specialist. It depends how many people you want to reach and in what area, but sometimes the new and specialist writers are more valuable.' This means that PR representatives are now engaging with a wider audience of gatekeepers and these range from celebrity figures with a significant online following to recreational blogs that attract an audience in a particular area. Brzezinska of Portland comments, 'The free option is always favourable as the client is already paying us a retainer.'

Are search and online reputation taking over?

As we saw, the 2014 Edelman Trust Barometer highlighted that online information is highly trusted by consumers. As part of the 2014 Digital News Report by the Reuters Institute,[6] data was collected about the most popular news brands – traditional and online. The work on brands found that 'audiences consume the majority of their online news from familiar and trusted brands'. However, there was an acknowledgement of the growing influence of search engines and 'increasingly varied ways to find that content' and the role of Google, Facebook, and other social media as 'intermediaries for a large proportion of news journeys online'.

One impact of the rise in popularity of search is the development of specialist online reputation management companies. Reputation management firms have been developed to assist with the growing reputation needs in the digital sphere. There has been a significant change in the way people consume information and there is a vital requirement by many companies and individuals to protect their reputation, specifically, their online reputation. Online reputation management is involved with how individuals are portrayed in the digital space and largely concerns the profile of an individual or company on search engines, such as Google. It differs to traditional reputation management because strategies have a significant technical component.

There is an increased awareness about the value of search engine results pages because they now play an important role in defining reputation. Individuals and companies are more conscious of their online profile and there is a merger of two different areas of expertise for a combined PR approach to the modern media world.

The need for reputation management can stem from negative news coverage, which now has greater longevity in the digital area. For example, a negative article about a historical incident may rank at the top of the first page of Google because the search engine's algorithm determines that it possesses a high degree of authority. It may be considered credible in the eyes of the search engine due to technical factors that mean it is highly optimised: yet algorithms can present a manipulated view of an individual or company. One key concern regards the accuracy of such content. For example, if the journalist made an error in the article or there is a certain agenda, the article may not be a fair reflection of the brand or individual, yet it still sits at the top of Google.

Search engines play a crucial role in defining reputation as a result of their search algorithms. There are often mistakes in these sources and these can cause irreparable damage. The case of Christopher Jefferies in the UK is an instructive example. He was suspected and arrested by the police investigating the murder in Bristol of Joanna Yeates in 2010, and vilified by the press. Despite being awarded significant compensation, his online profile is still littered with tabloid front pages and commentary associating him with the murder. The internet does not forget.

The idea that a search engine provides a profile of individuals that includes out-of-date, irrelevant, and inaccurate information has always been a concern for privacy issues. A landmark ruling in May 2014 saw the European Court back the 'right to be forgotten' in a case relating to a Spanish man who complained that Google's links to an auction notice for his repossessed home infringed his privacy. The ruling has opened a can of worms; it has been reported that a convicted paedophile and a politician were among those who subsequently asked to 'be forgotten'. Discussions have also revolved around censorship, matters of public interest, and the challenges of evaluating requests. However, the ruling is symbolic of a move to protect the privacy of private individuals.

One of the reasons that online reputation has become so important is because there is an increased volume of consumers using search as their first port of call when looking for information. Furthermore, many internet users do not venture further than the first page of results.

Search engine optimisation challenges algorithms in place and ORM also uses similar techniques. While there are exceptions to the rule, in most instances it is not possible to guarantee that a search engine is portraying a fair and balanced view without additional support. Individuals often need advice on the types of online assets they require and how best to position these assets. For example, an individual may need a company website, personal website, and additional social media assets.

Wikipedia can also be a concern. Wikipedia is a source of information that can be changed by anyone and also has certain requirements as to which type of sources can be used to support the profile.

News stories are considered an important source of validation for statements on Wikipedia. Wikipedia assumes that news articles are fair and accurate; it therefore allows these to be used as an endorsement of certain facts. However, varying agendas of publications and/or mistakes in news reporting can pose problems. It also does not advocate paid edits and a proposal earlier this year to facilitate the acceptance of such changes was rejected by Wikipedia on the grounds that it would not follow their principles.

Yet it is not uncommon for inaccurate information to be documented in Wikipedia and for it to be given a high priority in a company or individual search profile. The same issue occurs in relation to the priority of news articles. Some will rank well for certain keywords but not necessarily portray a balanced or fair view of the individual or company. In extreme cases, this can be highly damaging.

There are instances whereby this biased portrayal can snowball. Journalists sourcing information for an article will Google certain search terms and often incorporate the resulting information into their articles. A permanent depiction of an individual is then created as the false stories escalate.

Is reputation now much more important than before – as many in public relations claim? Dave King, CEO of Digitalis Reputation, argues there has not been an increase in awareness. He thinks instead that technology merely emphasises its importance.

> Organisations and individuals have less control and this is the main reason that reputation has become high on the agenda. The internet has empowered peer-reviewed content and this has changed the dynamics of trust. There is less trust in the media and there has never been much trust in PR. However, the internet acts as a platform that can showcase peer-reviewed content and this is becoming the most trusted of all.

Peer-reviewed content is most common when websites and newspapers enable live comments to be left underneath articles, creating a two-way information feed. Social media also enable peer-reviewed material, probably one of the most influential aspects of all. Articles, features, and reviews are now endorsed and shared among a much wider audience. This has an impact on the authority of media outlets and gives influence to those which were not originally considered to be powerful. Social sharing and peer-reviewed content has enabled new media brands to develop, such as the Huffington Post – the American news aggregator and blog was acquired by AOL in 2011 for $315m.

Says King:

> *Peer-reviewed content has very high levels of trust and that is why we have seen such growth in websites like Mumsnet. We are seeing the opportunity for specialist media to develop, which is driven by the readership and trust opportunities that can be found from trusted sources in a similar demographic, especially when it comes to considering the product service. Social media endorsement is also highly valued and the purchase cycle has been extended so that reviews form an important part of purchases.*

This is one aspect that PRs cannot influence. While they may have the ability to react and set certain news agendas, PR cannot interfere with the genuine customer response to a product – and consumers are wise to this fact. However, PRs can and do act to encourage and influence the conversation.

In sum

Public relations had a much easier landscape to tackle before the digital revolution, with the traditional press the main target. Although headlines could be powerful, their impact on reputation was typically briefer.

To use the parlance favoured by UK commentators: 'Today's news is tomorrow's chip wrapping' no longer works as a comfort to those 'monstered' by a tabloid, leaving reputation more fragile than ever before. This is partly due to news coverage and online reports providing broader and more sustained coverage. PR professionals have a varied landscape to tackle and more information to manage. There are also more voices to address and a larger amount of influencers.

This new landscape means that it is much harder to cover up stories, difficult to spin stories, and almost impossible to deter negative press. On the other hand, the communications industry – stretching from PR to brand marketing – now has many more routes to the end-consumer of its messaging.

In turn, this is leading to a more transparent approach to communications and demands a high level of strategic input, as well as a multifaceted approach. Although a more authentic approach is championed for corporate reputation, PR teams are also exploring new opportunities to gain press coverage for their clients; as we have seen, these methods are not always ethical.

With a revenue model that is probably more secure than media reliance on advertising or subscribers, PR is the sector with better near-term survival prospects. But that survival depends on being part of a food chain in which the media is a vital, if increasingly malnourished, component.

PR may therefore appear a more dynamic industry than the media on which it has long relied. We have emphasised the part that transparency plays, and it is a reasonable argument that PR professionals have simply become acutely aware of the new landscape that is emerging and have adapted behaviour to fit its demands. PR professionals have seen that they are unable to hide beneath the radar or manipulate stories and therefore advise clients to be more open and responsive than before. In doing so, they have turned the new order to their advantage – claiming that this means there is a vital need for PR to advise and consult on the communications approach, since mistakes in the exposed environment are more aggressively punished than ever before. PR came into being, in part, as a mechanism of defence: as in the sphere of national defence, when weapons of attack modernise, so do the weapons which defend.

This is leading to a new ecosystem in which companies, celebrities, politicians, brands, and campaigners are experimenting with new information tools. The old media hierarchy – literally intermediating between information and audiences – has been disrupted. Even in an analogue world, as we have shown, the 'wages of spin' were deployed aggressively to secure certain favourable message outcomes, particularly in politics. But in the analogue era, real impact still depended on PR ability to secure favourable coverage in different types of media, which was often disinclined to be fed pre-baked versions of events.

Today, the media and PR machines in our society are recalibrating their relationships. They are learning to coexist in a new disintermediated environment. Neither side can exercise power as they did in the past. Both communities – for so long interdependent – are competing on a much more crowded playing field. On this new field, it is not yet clear who will emerge on the winning side.

5

PR Elsewhere

Public relations and political communications are worldwide industries. In nearly all states except the very poor, public relations has established beachheads, more or less large and influential, a mixture, usually, of foreign and native companies.

Many of their techniques are similar. Guarding a CEO's reputation, getting journalists interested in a project, organising a fashion show, all call for roughly common approaches, adjusted for local customs and sensitivities. The differences are in the contexts within which they work: and much of that depends on the political system. This is, naturally, especially the case for political communications: but the system will also determine how free or constrained corporate public relations, both in-house teams and agencies, are in promoting their clients – and which clients they promote.

There is a study to be done on where and how public relations of all types has spread through the world, and what changes it brings in its wake. This is not it. Here we want to look briefly at three other PR cultures – those of China, of Russia, and of France – to bring out some of the differences between them and the Anglo-American cultures we have concentrated on. China is a one-party state; Russia is what its leaders called a 'managed' democracy; and France is a democracy. They were chosen to express different sorts of contrasts to the two largest Anglo-Saxon centres which think of themselves as the leaders in this area. They are probably still right to do so, but the global competition, here as everywhere, is becoming more intense.

China

Public relations, as an integral part of the twentieth-century capitalist economy and of democratic politics, could only be accepted as a practice and as an academic discipline within China in the 1980s, after Deng Xiao Peng's reforms had been securely embedded in the Party's lexicon and could be recognised by the state. It developed quickly: the first Western textbook, *An Introduction to Public Relations* was published in 1986; the Chinese International Public Relations Association was founded in 1991; in 1994, the Sun Yat-Sen University began to teach a course in PR; by 2005 an estimated[1] 30,000 people worked in PR and in 2007 all civil servants were told to familiarise themselves with public relations techniques.

In a fine essay, Anne Marie Brady (2009) writes that, after the 14th Party Congress in 1992 – the Congress at which the country was formally designated as a market economy – the then Party General Secretary Jiang Zemin gave increased powers to the propaganda department: 'for professional propagandists, the challenge was to organize propaganda and thought work suitable for the market economy and for China's unique political system' – a huge project for any PR.

In 2012, at its biannual congress, the head of the Information Office of the State Council Zhao Qizheng told the delegates that much still had to be done to 'realize the reality between the public opinion of China and the real China' – a job, he said, for PR.[2]

There is inevitably a tension between the needs of a developing authoritarian state and the theory and practice of PR, founded and largely developed in the US, a capitalist democracy. Zhao sees public relations as a tool for putting across to the world the image of China which the state leaders wish to convey. Western states also use public relations to project national images: but the activity is relatively modest.

China, by contrast, exerts strong control over the country's media, believing that only by such control can the country develop harmoniously – a concept taken from Confucianism, now much in vogue.

A Chinese TV correspondent, who did not wish to be named, said that even after the substantial privatisations and liberalisations of the news media in the 1980s, all media, especially television, remain strongly controlled. The many TV channels – four at national level (all CCTV: one for education, one for weather, one for broadcasting abroad, leaving CCTV with a domestic monopoly on national and international news and current affairs), 40 at provincial level, 364 at prefectural level and nearly 2,000 at county level – must take their cue from CCTV, which will often decree what news can be run. The correspondent said that 'local TV stations are often very restricted and neglected' – though they are encouraged by local administrations to send stories to CCTV for possible airing which reflect well on the local administrations and party committees.

The correspondent described a top-heavy bureaucracy at CCTV, with editors and news executives able to intervene at any stage in reporting and editing of material, with the Foreign Ministry and Publicity Department particularly keeping a close watch on what is broadcast.

A meeting in the early evening each day discusses the line to be taken in main stories: issues which cannot be covered except on explicit instructions include the Dalai Lama, the Tiananmen Square events, scandals surrounding the top leaders and their families, most dissidents, the Falun Gong sect, and freedom of religious belief. Other subjects – such as mass incidents (strikes and protests), political reform, corruption, independence movements (as in Tibet and Xinjiang) – can only be covered after careful negotiation with the censors.

The correspondent said that, while there are many ambitious and talented journalists and some 'honourable' programmes, the 'long list of stories we can't cover' produces 'a culture in which there is very little independence ... professionalism is less important than the bureaucracy, which is the essence of the system'.

This care taken by the authorities to produce coverage which conforms to the goals and ideology of the leadership is a vast exercise in political communications, which has the advantage for the leadership of having a monopoly on political power, with a monopoly national TV service and relatively tight control over media at every level.

The choice of what to show and how to show it; the layers of bureaucracy dedicated only partly to producing good television, partly to ensuring its conformity; the daily ensuring that lines, new and old, are adhered to – these are very far from the violent and arbitrary system which operated for the Maoist period, which penalised the slightest deviation from the then current line and which exerted the strictest orthodoxy over all media. Ruthless punishment of deviations has been replaced by guidance of the vast population into (by historic standards) a relatively broad path of social harmony as interpreted by an enlightened leadership. Those in journalism who stray too far are punished, by recent historical standards, very lightly – reprimanded, demoted, fired, and only occasionally imprisoned.

The authorities' position conforms to that of Bernays – the leaders explicitly 'engineer consent' and see it as one of their major responsibilities, promoting identity of interest not just between capital and labour, but between rulers and ruled, between different ethnicities, and between the now sharply diverging social classes. They would agree with Bernays – much studied by those interested in public relations in China, as is Walter Lippmann – in approving the view that 'our elected government officials … try to engineer our consent through the network of communications open to them'. Only the 'elected' would be cavilled at by the Chinese authorities.

Anne-Marie Brady comments:

> in the years since 1989, in a remarkable and unprecedented process of cultural exchange, China's propaganda system has deliberately absorbed the methodology of political public relations, mass communications, social psychology and other modern methods of mass persuasion commonly used in Western democratic societies, adapting them to Chinese conditions and needs … in doing so, China has also undergone a shift in what constitutes political authority.

The limits imposed by this attitude to governance are absolute: nothing is more important than the promotion of harmony. The less the authorities have relied on coercion, the more they have treated news and current affairs as a public relations exercise, a daily narrative spun from contemporary events – one meant in part for information, but also as a kind of daily reminder of the limits within which public debate is permitted. Public relations at the level of the firm can operate in a similar fashion to PR elsewhere – though the new mantra of PR in the West, that mistakes should be frankly and quickly admitted, finds itself at odds with a mindset which has tended to disguise mistakes and suppress past horrors. But the real relations with the public, those between the Chinese authorities and the mass of people, have largely served the former so far and will continue to do so.

Russia

This was written in spring 2014, when relations between Russia and the West were frigid because of Russia's capture of the Ukrainian province of Crimea, and its pressure on the Ukrainian government; yet even when they were better, there was little reliance, in government communications, on Western advice. President Vladimir Putin and his entourage have learned to take political communications in-house, to great effect. Where corporate PR tends to base itself on the same models worldwide, political PR is shaped by the political system, and differs greatly from country to country.

In the commercial sphere, the newly privatised companies as well as the wholly or largely state-owned corporations are enthusiastic users of public relations; most of the large Western agencies have offices in Russia. But public relations in Russia shares the problem (for Westerners) which is common, if in differing ways, to China (above) and India: that is, the continuing strength of the habit of settling issues through personal relationships. The impersonal, transaction-based relationships which underpin commercial and government dealings in the West are now more common in Moscow and St Petersburg, but even there they are subject to and usually trumped by networks of connections, friendships, and favours – a thick and so far resistant carpet of understandings which cover most public business.

In a survey of how public affairs are managed in contemporary Russia, Jason Jarrell, head of international relations at the Public Affairs Council and a former public affairs consultant in Russia, says that 'Russian society still fundamentally operates on an economy of favours, which is in part an outgrowth of the Soviet period, when monetary payments didn't have any intrinsic value. This makes having a meaningful network of contacts all the more important. There's even a common slang word for it: *blat*' (Judd 2013). Daria Ulantseva, a public affairs consultant who headed up government relations in Russia for Lafarge, the world's largest cement manufacturer, says that, in Moscow, 'if you work with government authorities, sometimes you can communicate via email, phone or letters. You don't have to meet them in person. But in the regions you absolutely have to meet them in person' (Judd 2013).

Blat was an 'outgrowth of the Soviet period', dependent on a largely non-monetised economy and intimately coiled round personal relationships of every kind. It has changed to fit the new semi-capitalist norms: Alena Ledeneva, the chronicler of Russia's 'informal' economy (which shades quickly into massive corruption), quotes an anonymous Novosibirsk businessman describing the new order of the late 1990s, in which he is prospering:

> *the forms of relationship maintained in blat networks did not disappear completely. All large-scale operations – financial swindles, non-paid loans, investment projects in which millions disappeared in unknown directions – are mostly based on former connections. Real business*

requires informal networks, even in the West. If old contacts turn bad, new but similar ones arise. What is changed is that the selection of people is more severe and the demands are harder. (1998)

The progress, as Western agencies would see it, towards a more transparent order has been slow because of the effectiveness of the *blat* networks; it is further slowed by the renationalisation of many of the large corporations, so that the Russian economy is now 60% state-owned or state-controlled – meaning that networks of influence within government at every level are now as important, even more important, than in the Soviet period. In that world, public relations can have some effect, but a limited one: and it is limited most of all by the dominance of the Kremlin. 'In Russia,' says Peter Necarsulmer, CEO of PBN-Hill and Knowlton Strategies in Moscow, 'your primary focus and radar are almost always on the presidential administration and key government bodies' (Judd 2013).

The story of the development of the Kremlin system through the 2000s and beyond is, in part, one of the refinements of an idea first mooted in the earliest days of Putin's presidency – that of 'managed democracy'. Managed democracy has parallels with the Chinese system (and the Chinese authorities, having viewed the collapse of the Soviet system and the relative chaos of the Yeltsin years with some contempt, now view the Putin-Russian developments with interest); it differs importantly in not resting on a monopolistic and still-powerful party present at every level of society, and, as is now clear, being tied to an increasingly explicit strategy of reconstructing Russia's sphere of influence/control over its neighbouring countries.

In the reconstruction, several figures became prominent, at least for a while. Marat Gelman, son of the well-known Soviet playwright and scriptwriter Alexander Gelman, and Gleb Pavlovsky, a former literary dissident who had been sentenced to three years' exile in the 1970s, founded a think tank named the Foundation for Effective Technologies, where they with a small group began to think through how Russia might be governed. Their influence on Putin and his circle is a matter of some dispute – Pavlovsky was credited with much power within the Kremlin in the early years, and happily spoke for it.

What is certain is that the idea of taking power back into the Kremlin – they called it 'sovereign', later 'managed' democracy – was followed; crucially, the Yeltsin-era oligarchs were either exiled, politically neutered, or – in the case of Mikhail Khodorkovsky, the boldest and richest – imprisoned. Pavlovsky and Gelman were both, as they said themselves, 'postmodernist' figures, flitting between the worlds of bohemia, the moderately liberal intelligentsia (Gelman later opened a smart art gallery), and the Kremlin. Pavlovsky worked in or near the Kremlin: Gelman was deputy head of Channel One Russia.

Gelman left first, in 2004, when Putin was triumphantly re-elected: in a 2012 interview,[3] he said that the experience of the election taught him that the new elite did not just want to win, they wanted to make sure no one else could win. Said Gelman: 'This so-called "sovereign democracy" lost all sense of shame. What happened was against my views – not only mine, but others' as well. We thought society could develop differently.'

Pavlovsky stayed on, though he was increasingly restive. In 2008, he wrote an essay in which he said that Russian TV was 'a drama with only one character [Putin]', and called for a wider choice of voices, including oppositionists. He got a rocket from Putin for that, and was dismissed three years later – returning to his dissident roots by joining the series of demonstrations and protests which flared in that year.

But Gelman and Pavlovsky had set a foundation on which others could build. They had made clear, especially to the TV directors, the line which should be followed: and if Pavlovsky jibbed against the 'one character' chasm into which Russian TV news and current affairs had fallen, he and Gelman could reflect ruefully that their belief that 'society could behave differently' was mistaken. Criticism of the government had been successfully confined to the liberal, even radical wing of the intelligentsia – who, as many of their number admitted, had lost almost all of their power, which had been at its height during the final years of the system many of them wished abolished, in the late Gorbachev Soviet period.

The most inventive of their successors, who came to exercise a grip of fascination on journalists, was Vladislav Surkov, a half-Chechen who in the late 1980s joined Mikhail Khodorkovsky's Menatep banking group, rising to become head of advertising, moving to Mikhail Fridman's Alfa Group, briefly filling the post of director of public relations for Channel One, then moving to be deputy chief of staff in the presidential administration in 1999, just as Putin was moving in, at the young age of 35. He gathered golden opinions from Khodorkovsky and his colleagues, pointing to his 'non-standard mindset' and glowing that 'every new step taken by this man is a sensation!' (Sakwa 2014).

Surkov took postmodernism to new levels. An admirer of Allen Ginsberg and the US beat poets, he developed a strong belief, which he often repeated to both domestic and foreign leaders and journalists, that – as he put it in a speech to a business forum in 2005 – 'there is no democracy in this country and the bureaucracy is ineradicable'. In an article published in 2009,[4] he argued that liberal reforms would lead to a collapse into chaos.

> *Even now when power is rather consolidated and ordered, many projects are very slow and difficult. If we add any sort of political instability to that then our development would simply be paralyzed. There would be a lot of demagoguery, a lot of empty talk, a lot of lobbying and ripping Russia to pieces, but no development [...] authority that is unconsolidated and unbalanced [and] weak democratic institutions are unable to ensure an economic revival.*

This was the mindset which governed social and media relations: Surkov used his high position to lay down the lines to be followed in a weekly meeting with the heads of the TV channels. He created a large group of young supporters of Putin who have been charged with acts of violence against dissidents and members of ethnic minorities; but most of his work was with the politicians and the media. He gathered many enemies: one of these was the oligarch Mikhail Prokhorov, whose presidential bid against Putin in 2012 saw him garner a little less than 8% of the vote, much of that in Moscow. He had become leader of a pro-business party Right Cause, and had been advised by Surkov; before the election, however, he denounced it as a 'puppet party' created by Surkov, saying that

> *I have felt on my own skin what a political monopoly is, when someone calls you every day and gives you all sorts of orders [...] there is a puppet master in this country who has privatized the political system. His name is Vladislav Surkov. As long as people like him control the process, politics is impossible.* (Aruntunyan 2014)

Surkov was demoted in late 2011, having leaned towards the departing president, Dmitry Medvedev, apparently concerned with the exchange of posts between president and prime minister which would allow Putin back into the Kremlin. He remained, however, a deputy prime minister and has since appeared to regain influence: he was among the first seven officials put under executive sanctions by President Obama in March 2014, after the taking of Crimea.

Surkov was one who, while assiduously serving the central power which he believed was the only bulwark against disorder, still sought to keep his options open – praising Yeltsin, Medvedev, and Putin, saying he had been privileged to serve all of them.

If he has a replacement in laying down the line, it is Dmitri Kiselev, a journalist of strongly nationalist views, who was in late 2013 appointed head of a new service, Russia Today, which under its previous chief, Svetlana Mironiuk, tried to hold a more or less objective line. Kiselev apparently has a mandate to excoriate the new Ukrainian government, the West, and the US in particular … and homosexuals.

His two most famed recent appearances were, first, in December 2013, when he told a chat show audience that 'I think that just imposing fines on gays for homosexual propaganda among teenagers is not enough. They should be banned from donating blood and sperm. And their hearts, in the case of an automobile accident, should be buried in the ground or burned as unsuitable for the continuation of life.' In a later broadcast, he accused Guido Westerwelle, the former German foreign minister who is gay, of an attempt to impose gay values on Ukraine.[5]

In March 2014, he mocked Barack Obama, accused him of supporting 'terrorists in Syria and fascists in Ukraine' and then while the screen showed a blasted, apparently post-nuclear strike scene, he said that Russia was the only country 'genuinely capable of turning the USA into radioactive ash'.

Kiselev operates in a harsher mode for harsher times – the present, as this is written. There is no longer any playing with postmodernist themes, any hint of disagreement with the policy of seizing and keeping Crimea while putting continuous pressure on the fragile Ukrainian government. Kiselev is a man for a season of war, able to employ reactionary and jingoistic tropes not because all in Russia agree with him, but because enough seem to – the studio audience happily applauded his sally on gays' hearts – and the Crimean seizure has over 90% public approval.

The Economist commented that Kiselev's appointment 'was a sign that Mr. Putin no longer sees any need to preserve even a veneer of European values […] it is also a sign of the extreme degradation of the Russian media'.[6] Beyond both of these, it was a sign that political communication in Russia, which had made some attempt to address and mediate among diverse groups in the society, had, at least for some time, ceased to play any such function.

France

Like much of the rest of continental Europe, the new, post-war techniques of intensive marketing, advertising, and public relations in France were largely based on US experience – as, to a more limited extent, they had been in the inter-war period. From the early 1950s, the first generation of teachers of publicity studied at marketing courses at the universities of Austin, Northwestern, and Harvard. Advertising and PR were both faced with sustained hostility in the radical 1960s and 1970s – where criticism of 'the manipulation of consumers, the creation of artificial needs, the illusions created by publicity, the lack of authenticity in modern life were charges leveled by [the literary theorist] Roland Barthes, the Situationist group and by [the sociologist] Jean Baudrillard' (Chessel 2004). The response was to concentrate on the practical values of marketing of all kinds, both to companies and to society; and in universities, to emphasise the quality of research and dispassionate scholarship of the field.

The radical, anti-capitalist, anti-American culture more prevalent in France than in most other Western states has remained strong, embedded in the political culture of both left and right. Political communication 'only gained traction in the 1980s, when TV ads began to replace posters as the main political communication tool' (Haag et al. 2011). Jacques Seguela, the best-known political communications executive in France, says:

> in 1978, three years before the 1981 [French presidential] campaign, there was no political communication consulting in France. Candidates had a campaign manager, who was not a professional, and who would call the fashionable advertisers of the day and ask them to make up a poster. The brief was: 'Make me a poster.' So, since we knew whether the candidate was left or right, we'd make a poster more to the left or more to the right, without even knowing what message they had or what their plans were. It was bullshit.

Seguela went on to advise, among others, Lionel Jospin – whom he says refused to be the actor in public which politicians must now be – and Nicolas Sarkozy, to whom he became close, admiring the former president for his activism and the speed with which he responded to events and even his 'bling' – saying on a TV show, 'How can you criticise a President for having a Rolex? In the end, everyone has a Rolex.' Seguela comes closest to being the inventor of political communications in France – again, on the Anglo-Saxon model: the colleague he most admires is the UK's Alastair Campbell. In 1969 he founded his own advertising, PR, and political communications agency, now owned by the advertising company Havas.

He did not advise Hollande, but has criticised him for his remark (before his election) that he 'hates the rich' and for his imposition of a 75% marginal tax rate on salaries over €1m.[7] He is, says Seguela, a man caught between the twentieth and twenty-first centuries – 'he hasn't understood the new generation, which is more interactive and better informed than that of their parents'. Hollande has been plagued by communications problems: in April, his communications adviser and main speechwriter, Aquilino Morelle, resigned after an investigation by the website Mediapart pointed to his continuing to lobby for the Danish pharmaceuticals company Lunbeck while working for IGAS, the public health inspection body. Details of a lavish lifestyle – consumption of expensive wines from the Versailles' palace cellars, three redecorations of his office – accompanied the piece.

The PR veteran's criticism reflects prevailing wisdom in global PR – at least for developed democratic states. Candidates must have a story, a theme, which is at the centre of their administration and to which all in it sign up; they must eschew anti-rich populism, since that conveys that they are 'anti-inspirational' and they must have a constant, active, and as far as possible 'personal' (or its appearance) presence on social media. There is, they believe, no 'exception Française' for French politics now.

Nor is there in corporate PR – up to a point. France, in spite of its much-advertised reluctance to embrace the free market, hosts one of the big four advertising-PR companies of the world. Marcel Bleustein-Blanchet founded Publicis in 1926 on US principles; in the mid-1930s, he bought a radio station, renamed it Radio Cité, introduced advertising jingles and Edith Piaf. As a Jew, his business was confiscated by the Nazis, and he joined the Resistance: he rebuilt Publicis after the war, made it a success, bequeathed it to Maurice Lévy in 1987 who boosted it into the third largest advertising company worldwide. In spring 2014, it attempted to merge with Omnicom, the second largest global firm after the UK's WPP – the merger did not take. Publicis's companies are mostly 'Anglo-Saxon' – including the UK's Saatchi & Saatchi and the US's Fallon Worldwide – and mainly advertising and marketing. Its main PR group, Publicis Consultants, is US based and specialises in representing healthcare clients.

Olivier Fleurot is the CEO of Publicis's strategic communications agency, MSLGroup, charged with building a global network of linked agencies. He works, he says, in a highly competitive environment – most of the big agencies have large offices in France – and the most lucrative part of corporate PR, finance, has a much weaker tradition in Paris than in London or New York.

He believes that the status of public relations has risen, but not to the levels it has attained in the US or UK.

> *The role of communications isn't yet as important as it is in the English-speaking world. You don't often see such a figure beside the CEO when he's giving an interview. CEOs – and ministers – have a slight sense of superiority in France: they expect to be able to speak and for everyone else to listen.*
>
> *Political consultancy is growing – but it's not systematic. It depends a lot on the relationships consultants and journalists had built with politicians. Communication is not as valued as it is in the US and the UK – it is, however, making progress.*

A key issue, Fleurot – a former CEO of the *Financial Times* – believes, has been that 'the media in France are nothing like as aggressive as they are in the UK. We don't have a powerful tabloid press.'

David Shriver, managing partner at the Tulchan Communications agency, worked for five years as a communications and strategy adviser to the CEO of the global supermarket chain Carrefour, fourth largest in the world. He says of the different media cultures:

> *there's a broad distrust of private business in France, but that's more of a cultural reflex – you see it more in political debate, as in Germany. The real difference between the UK and France is also that between the UK and the rest of Europe.*
>
> *When [the Belgian businessman] Luc Vandevelde became chairman of Marks & Spencer [2000–2004] he didn't believe the level of attacks on him – but being chairman of M&S is like being head of the national football team – it goes with the territory. It's not that way at all in France. There never really was any challenge to Carrefour. A similar company of the size and importance [in the UK] would have to deal with a level of scrutiny much greater. But I came to believe that the UK media – the English-language media in general – do keep companies honest in a way that doesn't happen in other countries.*

This is changing: Fleurot says, 'Look at Mediapart of Edwy Plenel [a former editorial director of *Le Monde*]. They were able to bring down the Budget Minister Jérôme Cahuzac after they showed he had a Swiss bank account, which he had denied. There's also *Canard Enchaîné*.' President Sarkozy, who revealed much of his private life and saw unwelcome revelations of much more, and President Hollande, who has suffered wholly unwelcome revelations of his private life, have both broken, willingly and unwillingly, the tradition of silence about the top politician's private life – or seen it broken for them by the media, especially by the internet and by social media.

In sum

- Authoritarian states keep tight control of political communication, and use a variety of propaganda techniques only occasionally challenged by media struggling for independence.
- Anglo-Saxon methods have conquered in corporate communications, at least for the moment. Public relations, political communications, and journalism all evolve, and the hegemony which (mainly) the US and also the UK, have exercised in the first two – less decisively in the third – will certainly change and develop. The advantage, apart from decades' experience of creativity, is in the English language; that is likely to last some time, but itself may, in time, lose out to other languages.
- The experience of the internet and social media shows that authoritarian states can control them to a degree, and can use them both to identify opponents and to insert more and more subtle propagandist narratives into the social sphere. However, in the long run, short of a totalitarian clampdown, the internet is likely to produce more openness and debate.

6

Conclusions and Recommendations

Public relations is booming at present, and its mechanisms and practices are being adopted by corporations and companies across the globe. Journalism in the developed world is undergoing a series of radical changes, and is available in a greater choice of forms than ever before. The first, however, is highly profitable: while newspaper, magazine, and some forms of broadcast journalism struggle to discover a stable model for making profits. This will not change soon.

Newspapers and magazines under pressure are thus pulling their editorial closer to public relations and advertising to secure funding, both in the carriage of native advertising and in using public relations narratives. The internet, which increasingly carries all media, blurs the distinctions which had taken physical form in the pre-digital era.

Much popular journalism, especially that concerned with celebrity, scandal, and sport, is increasingly mixed in with commercial and other messages. The need for new income streams is creating a new kind of editor-cum-chief-executive, who oversees both the editorial and the commercial sides of the news organisation.

More specialised journalism – on political, legal, scientific issues and on foreign affairs – is being organised into niches. This kind of 'serious' journalism will continue to exist for the foreseeable future on public broadcasters and in those upmarket newspapers which continue to be viable; but the future seems more and more likely to be a highly different one. Where they do not have foundation funding or cannot generate enough income from a pay wall, these niches will attract sponsorship from corporations which wish to be associated with the kind of content they produce. This will raise new questions of independence.

The greater reliance of corporations on public relations will continue to increase the importance of the practitioners; they will develop further the trend of bringing the production of content into more and more corporate activities, using journalistic techniques and tropes to do so.

More and more journalists will be employed in the growing world which exists between PR and journalism.

Political communication will also become more pervasive and powerful, as the leading politicians become more dependent on presentation, polling evidence, and direct connectivity with their followers through social media. Parties, already much weaker, will weaken further – as will the already fuzzy lines between different political ideologies.

The techniques of political communication, and of corporate PR, will increasingly be adopted by a wider spectrum of states, including authoritarian states. This need not be uniformly sinister: the experience of political communicators working in states where the democratic institutions are new and raw shows that bringing politicians into closer touch with the demands and problems of their fellow citizens can produce a greater understanding of the need for responsiveness, and for policies and programmes to deliver improvements. However, PR techniques can also be adapted to exclude political communication and to draw populations closer to the ruling group or party by targeting external or internal enemies and threats.

The overall trend evident in all these developments is towards a much more fluid media environment than we have seen before, where many roles in the production of content are no longer to be sharply distinguished from each other. This does not signify the 'death' of journalism; on the contrary, journalism gives every sign of being more vital, interesting and richer than at any previous time. It does mean, however, that new relationships between those who sponsor journalism and those who produce it must now be negotiated – and are being negotiated.

The overall recommendation is for journalism to retain its autonomy as the end product of these renegotiations (which will in practice be never-ending). Journalism must continue to find ways of providing coherent narratives about the world which illuminate its workings and give citizens an understanding of how their life is governed, and how they can best play a meaningful part in society. The new digital media world allows many more ways of securing these aims than before: there is no reason why the new relationships between journalists and the money they need to follow cannot be more socially useful than in the past.

Appendix: List of Interviewees (Who Agreed to be Named)

Tim Allan, Portland Communications
Tim Bell, Bell Pottinger
Paul Blanchard, Right Angles
Mark Bolland, Mark Bolland Associates
Anne-Marie Brady, University of Canterbury
Gosia Brzezinska, Portland Communications
Colin Byrne, Weber Shandwick
Alastair Campbell, Communications Consultant
Andrew Caesar-Gordon, Electric Airwaves
Sumeet Desai, Head of Public Affairs RBS
Max Dundas, Dundas Communications
Richard Edelman, Edelman
Olivier Fleurot, MSLGroup
Phil Hall, PHA Media
John Harris, Politico
Dave King, Digitalis Reputation
Joe Lockhart, Communications Consultant
Mike McCurry, Public Strategies Washington
Kevin Madden, Communications Consultant
Mark Malloch Brown, FTI Consulting
Calvin Mitchell, Credit Suisse
Dick Morris, Politico
Vanessa Neill, Credit Suisse
Pete Pedersen, Grayling
Robert Phillips, Jericho Chambers
George Pitcher, Jericho Chambers
Paul Polman, Unilever
Ruby Quince, Freud Communications

Roland Rudd, RLM Finsbury

Deborah Saw, Former Managing Director of Citigate Dewe Rogerson Corporate, now at Newgate

David Shriver, Tulchan Communications

Jake Siewert, Goldman Sachs

James Thomlinson, Bell Pottinger Wired

Simon Walker, Institute of Directors

Ed Williams, Edelman UK

Notes

Introduction

1 Alastair Campbell, 'Why the World of PR is Changing', *Huffington Post* (27 June 2013): http://www.huffingtonpost.co.uk/alastair-campbell/pr-world-is-changing_b_3511449.html.

Chapter 1   Public Relations: A Brief Selective History

1 Dennis Hevesi, 'Daniel J. Edelman, a Publicity Pioneer, Dies at 92', *New York Times* (15 January 2013): www.nytimes.com/2013/01/16/business/daniel-j-edelman-a-publicity-pioneer-dies-at-92.html.

Chapter 2   Corporate PR

1 http://worldreport.holmesreport.com.
2 '2014 PR Trend Forecast' (31 January 2014): http://www.holmesreport.com/featurestories-info/14559/2014-PR-Trend-Forecast.aspx.
3 Richard Edelman, 'Sir Martin Sorrell's View on the Future of Marketing Services' (16 April 2014): http://www.edelman.com/p/6-a-m/sir-martin-sorrells-view-future-marketing-services.
4 Alexandra Bruell, 'Weber Shandwick Sets Up New Unit to Capitalize on Content Marketing Craze' (27 March 2013): http://adage.com/article/agency-news/weber-shandwick-sets-unit-capitalize-content-marketing-craze/240564/.
5 Michael Sebastian, 'Five Things to Know About The New York Times' New Native Ads' (8 January 2014): http://adage.com/article/media/york-times-debuts-native-ad-units-dell/290973.
6 'Guardian Labs; Death or rebirth of news media?' (20 February 2014): http://www.hkstrategies.co.uk/shocks-and-stares/posts/2014/february/20/guardian-labs-death-or-rebirth-of-news-media.aspx.
7 Ken Auletta, 'Jill Abramson and the Times: What Went Wrong?', *The New Yorker* (15 May 2014): http://www.newyorker.com/online/blogs/newsdesk/2014/05/jill-abramson-and-the-times-what-went-wrong.html.

8 'We are all in PR now', *British Journalism Review* (5 June 2010): http://www.bjr.org. uk/blog/2010/06/05/we-are-all-in-pr-now.

9 'The ultimate launch? Microsoft turns Lichtenstein's landmarks into a futuristic world for launch of new Halo Xbox game', *Mail Online* (31 October 2012): http:// www.dailymail.co.uk/sciencetech/article-2225733/Microsoft-turns-Lichtensteins-landmarks-futuristic-world-launch-new-Halo-Xbox-game.html.

10 Alex Black, '1983–2008: So what's changed?', *PR Week* (15 September 2008): http:// www.prweek.com/article/846144/1983---2008-so-what's-changed.

11 'McKinsey conversations with global leaders: Paul Polman of Unilever' (October 2009): http://www.mckinsey.com/insights/strategy/mckinsey_conversations_with_ global_leaders_paul_polman_of_unilever.

12 http://www.citizenrenaissance.com.

13 Marc Wright, 'HSBC exchanges top down for listening': http://www.simply-communicate.com/case-studies/company-profile/hsbc-exchanges-top-down-listening.

14 Patrick Radden Keefe, 'Buried Secrets', *The New Yorker* (8 July 2013): http://www. newyorker.com/magazine/2013/07/08/buried-secrets?

15 David Hencke, Mark Watts, Martin Hickman and Alex Varley-Winter, 'Transcript: Rupert Murdoch recorded at meeting with Sun staff' (2 July 2013): http://www.exaronews.com/articles/5026/transcript-rupert-murdoch-recorded-at-meeting-with-sun-staff.

Chapter 3   Political Communications

1 Adam Liptak, Supreme Court Strikes Down Overall Political Donation Cap', *New York Times* (2 April 2014): www.nytimes.com/2014/04/03/us/politics/supreme-court-ruling-on-campaign-contributions.html.

2 Stephen Braun and Jack Gillum, '2012 Presidential Election Cost Hits $2 Billion Mark', *Huffington Post* (6 December 2012): www.huffingtonpost. com/2012/12/06/2012-presidential-election-cost_n_2254138.html.

3 Jayati Ghosh, 'Narendra Modi and the BJP bludgeoned their way to election victory', *The Guardian* (16 May 2014): http://www.theguardian.com/commentisfree/2014/ may/16/narendra-modi-bjp-election-victory-aggression-campaign-india.

4 Jill Lepore, 'The Lie Factory', *The New Yorker* (24 September 2012): http://www. newyorker.com/reporting/2012/09/24/120924fa_fact_lepore.

5 Eric Alterman, 'G.O.P. Chairman Lee Atwater: Playing Hardball', *New York Times* (30 April 1989): www.nytimes.com/1989/04/30/magazine/gop-chairman-lee-atwater-playing-hardball.html.

6 Ezra Klein, 'How politics makes us stupid' (6 April 2014): http://www.vox. com/2014/4/6/5556462/brain-dead-how-politics-makes-us-stupid.

7 Michael Wolff, 'Ezra Klein, Glenn Greenwald and the odd rise of personal brand journalism', *The Guardian* (6 January 2014): http://www.theguardian.com/ commentisfree/2014/jan/06/ezra-klein-leave-washington-post-personal-brand.

8 'Our vision for the new SCOTUSblog' (4 September 2010): www.scotusblog. com/2010/09/about-scotusblog-4-0.

9 'Between Two Ferns with Zach Galifianakis: President Barack Obama' [video interview] (11 March 2014): http://www.funnyordie.com/videos/18e820ec3f/between-two-ferns-with-zach-galifianakis-president-barack-obama.

10 Michael D. Shear, 'Obama's New Approach Takes a Humorous Turn', *New York Times* (10 March 2014): http://www.nytimes.com/2014/03/11/us/politics/obamas-new-approach-takes-a-humorous-turn.

11 Jay Rosen, 'Everything That's Wrong with Political Journalism in One Washington Post Item' (5 August 2012): http://pressthink.org/2012/08/everything-thats-wrong-with-political-journalism-in-one-washington-post-item.

12 Eyder Peralta, 'Guy On Train Live Tweets Former CIA Chief's On-Background Interview' (24 October 2013): www.npr.org/blogs/thetwo-way/2013/10/24/240587739/guy-on-train-live-tweets-former-nsa-chiefs-on-background-interview.

13 Ken Auletta, 'Fortress Bush', *The New Yorker* (19 January 2004): www.newyorker.com/archive/2004/01/19/040119fa_fact_auletta.

14 Santiago Lyon, 'Obama's Orwellian Image Control', *New York Times* (11 December 2013): www.nytimes.com/2013/12/12/opinion/obamas-orwellian-image-control.html.

15 Leonard Downie Jr and Sara Rafsky, 'The Obama Administration and the Press' (10 October 2013): http://cpj.org/reports/2013/10/obama-and-the-press-us-leaks-surveillance-post-911.php.

16 James Surowiecki, 'Punditonomics', *The New Yorker* (7 April 2014): www.newyorker.com/talk/financial/2014/04/07/140407ta_talk_surowiecki.

17 Andrew Beaujon, 'Risen: Obama administration is this generation's "greatest enemy of press freedom"' (24 March 2014): http://www.poynter.org/latest-news/mediawire/244525/risen-obama-administration-is-this-generations-greatest-enemy-of-press-freedom.

18 David Shribman, 'Congress; Mail on tax withholding yields bonanza of names', *New York Times* (4 May 1983): http://www.nytimes.com/1983/05/04/us/congress-mail-on-tax-withholding-yields-bonanza-of-names.html.

19 Joel Makower, 'Exit Interview: Leslie Dach, Walmart' (15 July 2013): www.greenbiz.com/blog/2013/07/15/exit-interview-leslie-dach-walmart.

20 Steve Coll, 'Gusher', *The New Yorker* (9 April 2012): www.newyorker.com/reporting/2012/04/09/120409fa_fact_coll.

Chapter 4 How it's Done: the Internet as a Mechanism for a Changed Relationship between PR and Journalism

1 Miles Osborne and Mark Dredze, 'Facebook, Twitter and Google Plus for Breaking News: Is There a Winner?' (last modified: 16 May 2014), AAAI Publications, 8th International AAAI Conference on Weblogs and Social Media: http://www.aaai.org/ocs/index.php/ICWSM/ICWSM14/paper/view/8072.

2 The Mail Online recorded 134 million unique browsers in July 2013 (confirmed by the Audit Bureau of Circulation on 22 Aug. 2013): http://www.journalism.co.uk/news/abc-confirms-mail-online-s-134m-web-traffic-for-july/s2/a553895.

3 Chelsea Varney, 'Celebrity Twitter Ads: Regulations, Allegations and Selling Out', *Business 2 Community* (9 October 2013): http://www.business2community.com/social-media/celebrity-twitter-ads-regulations-allegations-selling-0642066.

4 Laura Stampler, 'The FTC is Sick of Celebrities Ignoring Rules for Sponsored Tweets', *Business Insider* (11 June 2013): http://www.businessinsider.com/celebrities-ignoring-ftc-rules-for-sponsored-tweets-2013-6#ixzz3CpQSptPX; the *New York Times*: http://bits.blogs.nytimes.com/2013/06/09/disruptions-celebrities-product-plugs-on-social-media-draw-scrutiny.

5 Hannah Furness, 'Wayne Rooney Reprimanded for Advertising Nike on Twitter', *The Telegraph* (20 June 2012): http://www.telegraph.co.uk/technology/twitter/9343349/Wayne-Rooney-reprimanded-for-advertising-Nike-on-Twitter.html.

6 'Pathways to News: How Audiences Discover News Online', *Digital News Report 2014*, Reuters: http://www.digitalnewsreport.org/survey/2014/pathways-to-news-2014.

Chapter 5 PR Elsewhere

1 Ai Zhang, 'Understanding Chinese Public Relations Education: A Critical and Cultural Perspective': http://drum.lib.umd.edu/bitstream/1903/10238/1/Zhang_umd_0117E_11055.pdf.

2 'China International Public Relations Association Congress Held in Beijing' (26 July 2012): http://english.cri.cn/6909/2012/07/26/2561s713817.htm.

3 Mark Mackinnon, 'A former Kremlin spin doctor rues his role in Putin's rise', *The Globe and Mail* (13 March 2012): www.theglobeandmail.com/news/world/a-former-kremlin-spin-doctor-rues-his-role-in-putins-rise/article533660.

4 Guy Faulconbridge, 'Kremlin warns against wrecking Russia with democracy', Reuters (26 October 2009): www.reuters.com/article/2009/10/26/us-russia-kremlin-idUSTRE59P3ZL20091026.

5 'Ukraine: Russia's chief propagandist', *The Economist* (10 December 2013): www.economist.com/blogs/easternapproaches/2013/12/ukraine.

6 'Ukraine: Russia's chief propagandist', *The Economist* (10 December 2013): www.economist.com/blogs/easternapproaches/2013/12/ukraine.

7 Julien Marion, 'Jacques Séguéla: François Holland "est dans une posture démagogique"' (30 May 2013): www.bfmtv.com/economie/jacques-seguela-francois-hollande-est-une-posture-demagogique-526230.html.

References

Anthony, Scott (2008) 'Stephen Tallents and the Development of Public Relations in Britain', D.Phil., Wolfson College, Oxford.

Arutunyan, Anna (2014) *The Putin Mystique* (Skyscraper).

Bernays, Edward (1947) 'The Engineering of Consent', *Annals of the American Academy of Political and Social Science*, 250 (March).

—— (2011) *Crystallizing Public Opinion* (Reprint edition, Ig Publishing).

Blick, Andrew (2004) *People Who Live in the Dark* (Politico's Publishing).

Boorstin, Daniel (1997) *The Image* (Vintage).

Brady, Anne-Marie (2009) 'Mass Persuasion as a Means of Legitimation and China's Popular Authoritarianism', *American Behavioural Scientist* (12 October), <http//abs.sagepub.com/content/53/3 /434>.

Brady, John (1997) *Bad Boy* (Allison Wesley).

Burt, Tim (2012) *Dark Art* (Elliott & Thompson).

Castells, Manuel (2009) *Communication Power* (OUP).

Chessel, Marie-Emanuelle (2004) 'L'enseignement de la publicité en France au XXe siècle', *Le Temps des Medias*, 1/2.

Frayn, Michael (2005) *Towards the End of the Morning* (Faber & Faber).

Goodwin, Doris Kearns (2013) *The Bully Pulpit: Theodore Roosevelt, William Howard Taft and the Golden Age of Journalism* (Simon & Schuster).

Haag, Christopher, Jean Francois Coget, and Tessa Melkonian (2011) 'Top Level Communication: Behind the Scenes with Jacques Seguela', *Organization Management Journal*, 8.

Halberstam, David (2000) *The Powers that Be* (University of Illinois Press Reprint editions).

Harding, James (2008) *Alpha Dogs* (Atlantic Books).

Jay, Douglas (1937) *The Socialist Case* (Faber & Faber).

Judd, Elizabeth (2013) *Russian Renaissance? Managing Public Affairs in Today's Russia* (Foundation for Public Affairs).

Klein, Joe (2007) *Politics Lost* (Broadway Books).

Ledeneva, Alena (1998) *Russia's Economy of Favours* (CUP).

Lippmann, Walter (1997) *Public Opinion* (Simon & Schuster Free Press Paperbacks).

Mair, Peter (2013) *Ruling the Void* (Verso).

Micklethwait, John and Adrian Wooldridge (2014) *The Fourth Revolution: the Global Race to Reinvent the State* (Penguin).

Moore, Martin (2006) *The Origins of Modern Spin* (Palgrave Macmillan).

Napolitan, Joe (1972) *The Election Game and How to Win it* (Doubleday).

Packard, Vance (2007) *The Hidden Persuaders* (Ig Publishing).

Patterson, Thomas (2013) *Informing the News* (Vintage).

Pitcher, George (2002) *Death of Spin* (John Wiley).

Sakwa, Richard (2014) *Putin and the Oligarch* (I.B.Tauris).

Schneider, John G. (1956) *The Golden Kazoo* (Rinehart & Co).

Shirky, Clay (2008) *Here Comes Everybody* (Allen Lane).

Tye, Larry (1998) *The Father of Spin* (Holt).

Viroli, Maurizio (2014) *Redeeming the Prince* (Princeton UP).

Westen, Drew (2007) *The Political Brain* (Public Affairs).

RISJ/I.B.TAURIS PUBLICATIONS

CHALLENGES

Journalism and PR: News Media and Public Relations in the Digital Age
John Lloyd and Laura Toogood
ISBN: 978 1 78453 062 4

Reporting the EU: News, Media and the European Institutions
John Lloyd and Cristina Marconi
ISBN: 978 1 78453 065 5

Transformations in Egyptian Journalism
Naomi Sakr
ISBN: 978 1 78076 589 1

Climate Change in the Media: Reporting Risk and Uncertainty
James Painter
ISBN: 978 1 78076 588 4

Women and Journalism
Suzanne Franks
ISBN: 978 1 78076 585 3

EDITED VOLUMES

Media and Public Shaming: The Boundaries of Disclosure
Julian Petley (ed.)
ISBN: 978 1 78076 586 0 (HB); 978 1 78076 587 7 (PB)

Political Journalism in Transition: Western Europe in a Comparative Perspective
Raymond Kuhn and Rasmus Kleis Nielsen (eds)
ISBN: 978 1 78076 677 5 (HB); 978 1 78076 678 2 (PB)

Transparency in Politics and the Media: Accountability and Open Government
Nigel Bowles, James T. Hamilton and David A. L. Levy (eds)
ISBN: 978 1 78076 675 1 (HB); 978 1 78076 676 8 (PB)

The Ethics of Journalism: Individual, Institutional and Cultural Influences
Wendy N. Wyatt (ed.)
ISBN: 978 1 78076 673 7 (HB); 978 1 78076 674 4 (PB)